OPPENHEIMER'S
CHOICE

SUNY SERIES IN PHILOSOPHY

George R. Lucas, Jr., editor

OPPENHEIMER'S

CHOICE

Reflections from Moral Philosophy

RICHARD MASON

STATE UNIVERSITY OF NEW YORK PRESS

Published by
STATE UNIVERSITY OF NEW YORK PRESS,
Albany

© 2006 State University of New York

For information, address State University of New York Press
194 Washington Avenue, Suite 305, Albany, NY 12210-2384

Production, Laurie Searl
Marketing, Michael Campochiaro

Library of Congress Cataloging-in-Publication Data

Mason, Richard, 1948-
   Oppenheimer's choice : reflections from moral philosophy / Richard Mason.
      p. cm. — (SUNY series in philosophy)
   Includes bibliographical references (p.   ) and index.
   ISBN 0-7914-6781-3 (hardcover : alk. paper)
   1. Technology—Moral and ethical aspects. 2. Ethics. 3. Oppenheimer, J. Robert, 1904-1967. I. Title. II. Series.

BJ59.M38 2006
170—dc22

2005020545

10 9 8 7 6 5 4 3 2 1

To Eline Tolstoy and Maya Tolstoy, scientists

Moral philosophy has, indeed, this peculiar disadvantage, which is not found in natural, that in collecting its experiments, it cannot make them purposely, with premeditation, and after such a manner as to satisfy itself concerning every particular which may arise. When I am at a loss to know the effects of one body upon another in any situation, I need only put them in that situation, and observe what results from it. But shou'd I endeavour to clear up after the same manner any doubt in moral philosophy, by placing myself in the same case with that which I consider, 'tis evident this reflection and premeditation wou'd so disturb the operation of my natural principles, as must render it impossible to form any just conclusion from the phænomenon. We must therefore glean up our experiments in this science from a cautious observation of human life, and take them as they appear in the common course of the world, by men's behaviour in company, in affairs, and in their pleasures. Where experiments of this kind are judiciously collected and compar'd, we may hope to establish on them a science, which will not be inferior in certainty, and will be much superior in utility to any other of human comprehension.

—Hume, A *Treatise of Human Nature*, Book I, Introduction

CONTENTS

INTRODUCTION

The aim of this book is to reflect on a course in life taken by one man—Robert Oppenheimer—and, more particularly, his choice to accept the leadership of research and development at Los Alamos between 1942 and 1945, which resulted in the production and use of the first atomic bombs.

The bare external facts of Oppenheimer's life can be stated straightforwardly.

He was born in New York City in 1904. His parents were Jewish; his father a first-generation immigrant from Germany, his mother from a family settled for some time in Baltimore. His father had prospered in business. The family was wealthy. Oppenheimer attended the Ethical Culture School from 1911 to 1921. After studies and research at Harvard, Cambridge, and Göttingen, and some postdoctoral work elsewhere, he settled into appointments at Berkeley and Caltech. He made a steady contribution to research in physics during the 1930s. By the early 1940s, he moved closer to the initial stages of the U.S. government's atomic program—later to be known as the Manhattan Project—and by the winter of 1942–1943 he had been appointed director of the research laboratory to be built at Los Alamos. The first atomic bomb was tested at Alamogordo on July 16, 1945: "Trinity." A uranium bomb was dropped on Hiroshima on August 6; a plutonium bomb on Nagasaki on August 9. The war ended six days later. Oppenheimer left Los Alamos in October 1945. After periods at Caltech and Berkeley, he became Director of the Institute for Advanced Study at Princeton. He served the Atomic Energy Commission in central advisory and consultative roles until 1954, when his security clearance was removed after hearings before the commission's Personnel Security Board. Oppenheimer remained at Princeton until shortly before his death in 1967. His security clearance was never reinstated.

A less impersonal narrative hardly needs to be more detailed. Oppenheimer was widely known as a reflective physicist. In his Princeton years he became a famous polymath. Some found him too reflective, dispersing his talents too widely for genuine creativity in a specialized and competitive field. His many public pronouncements after 1945 were thoughtful, well-informed, and perceptive. But it is not as an original thinker or writer that we look to him now. He remains interesting because he did what he did with his eyes open, and not because he left us any intellectualized record of strenuous decision-making. At the security hearings in 1954 there was a grueling interrogation of his motives and intentions in the early 1940s, but such retrospective analysis, especially in such a fraught context, must be treated with caution. Even the debates among atomic scientists in the late 1940s, before the worst Cold War paranoia took hold, were more openly reflective, in very different circumstances, than whatever went through the minds of Oppenheimer and his colleagues from 1942 to 1944, when the priority was action, not words.[1]

There are excellent studies of Oppenheimer's contribution at Los Alamos and of his later security problems. His later conclusions on atomic weapons have been subjected to much scrutiny, some of it sharply critical.[2] This book will reflect on how he came to work on the bomb, what this meant and what it means now. So the aim is not biographical and it is not psychological. There will be no startling revelations and there will be no speculations on conscious or unconscious motives. One of the advantages in dealing with Oppenheimer is that we do not have to wrestle with soul-searching or hesitation. His decision in 1942 is not of interest because it felt a difficult one for him. On the contrary, he moved swiftly into his work on the bomb and pursued it with single-minded zeal. There were many doubts among those who worked at Los Alamos, particularly as the war in Europe was ending, but he drove on to the conclusion. We need to ponder the outcome of his initial choices, his subsequent actions and their context, not a record of his thoughts.

Oppenheimer himself claimed that the atomic project was a technical challenge, rather than a problem in pure science. That was both modest and misleading. For now, it is worth noting that his later wartime contribution went well beyond the building of the bomb, and into its use. From his security hearings:

ROBB: In fact, Doctor, you testified, did you not, that you assisted in selecting the target for the drop of the bomb on Japan?

OPPENHEIMER: Right.

ROBB: You knew, did you not, that the dropping of that atomic bomb on the target you had selected will kill or injure thousands of civilians, is that correct?

OPPENHEIMER: Not as many as turned out.

ROBB: How many were killed or injured?

OPPENHEIMER: 70,000.

ROBB: Did you have moral scruples about that?

OPPENHEIMER: Terrible ones.

ROBB: But you testified the other day, did you not, sir, that the bombing of Hiroshima was very successful?

OPPENHEIMER: Well, it was technically successful.

ROBB: Oh, technically.

OPPENHEIMER: It is also alleged to have helped end the war.[3]

The responsibility for the use of the first atomic bombs in 1945, and the selection of targets, was diffuse. The drive behind the creation of the first bombs was surprisingly narrow. General Leslie R. Groves, who knew better than anyone, as the military head of the entire project, spoke frankly at the 1954 hearings:

GARRISON: You appointed Dr. Oppenheimer to be the director of the work at Los Alamos?

GROVES: Yes, sir.

GARRISON: You devolved great responsibility upon him?

GROVES: Yes.

GARRISON: Would you just say a word about the nature of that responsibility?

GROVES: Complete responsibility for the operation of Los Alamos Laboratory, the mission of which was to carry on the research necessary to develop the design of a bomb, to develop the probabilities of whether a bomb was possible, and if the design would be feasible, and to develop what the power of the bomb would be. . . .

GARRISON: How would you rate the quality of his achievement as you look back on it?

GROVES: Naturally I am prejudiced, because I selected him for the job, but I think he did a magnificent job as far as the war effort was concerned . . .[4]

Groves concluded in his memoirs that the United States could only have produced the atomic bomb in time of war "because of the great costs and difficulties involved and the apparently very small chance of success." The project had employed 600,000 people on the tightest of deadlines. No one can say that it would not have succeeded without Oppenheimer. We can say that it would not have worked as and when it did without him; and that is to say a great deal. "I have never felt that it was a mistake to have selected and cleared Oppenheimer for his wartime post," wrote Groves, "he accomplished his assigned mission and he did it well. We will never know whether anyone else could have done it better or even as well. I do not think so, and this opinion is almost universal among those who were familiar with the wartime operations at Los Alamos."[5]

But why a book like this about Oppenheimer?

His choice in 1942, and his work from then until 1945, represents something of permanent importance. The Manhattan Project was the first huge scientific-military-industrial-financial undertaking, with obviously large consequences. Oppenheimer mattered in a way that most people do not matter. His choices and actions made a difference to the world. This may be how it is for some people, but for most it is not so and never will be. That sounds uncomfortable, but it leads to some central problems discussed in this book: about the particular place of a scientist in society—problems about responsibility, the place of curiosity, about the relation between theory and practice. A notion of specialized scientific ethics seems at the same time repugnant and absolutely necessary. Oppenheimer's choice leads to questions about corporate action and responsibility that still face scientists today and can only become more acute. A large technical and industrial project with an equally intricate political superstructure could never be the responsibility of one person. What does this mean for choice, guilt, blame, and conscience? Are these concepts simply left over from an older, simpler world?

Much has been written about the Holocaust in Europe, where responsibility may be pinned on people of undeniable evil who lost a war. Whatever the intentions of political leaders in wartime, most of those who take part in wars, and who suffer the consequences, are motivated less by malice or hatred than by patriotism, solidarity, or some feeling for self-protection. In the future, it seems far less probable that an important industrial power will fall under the spell of a malevolent dictator than that wars may start as a result of misalliances, confusion, or political misunderstanding. The creation of atomic weapons was the responsibility of people in a free society whose initial intentions could hardly be seen as evil, yet the consequences for Hiroshima and Nagasaki were as dreadful as any of the destruction during the war in Europe. How this came about, especially in its first steps, merits some careful thought.

Freedom of choice, in a free society, is relevant. The case of Werner Heisenberg in Nazi Germany, in contrast, raises its own questions. Heisenberg chose not to leave his country and to work with some degree of commitment on the development of atomic weapons in time of war. Not surprisingly, the exact degree of his commitment and the reasons for his actions have been the subjects of the most detailed debate.[6] In the Soviet Union, Andrei Sakharov followed some way along Oppenheimer's path through the development of nuclear weapons, and later went far further in his repudiation of the bomb, at the greatest personal cost. In his memoirs he noted tersely: "In 1948, no one asked whether or not I *wanted* to take part in such work. I had no real choice in the matter."[7] In contrast, Oppenheimer's choice is of particular interest because it was unforced. He could have refused Groves's offer to lead the project. He could have taken some contributory part, or no part at all. This might have been true of Heisenberg, too. Maybe he could have assumed no part in German atomic research or he could have lied about its practicability at no loss or danger to himself; but in his case the uncertainties are complicating. If Sakharov had tried to refuse the role offered to him in

1948, most probably he would have been shot. Oppenheimer could never have wanted to claim that he had to do what he did. Nor—as with Groves, for example, as a serving military officer, (I. I. Rabi called him "that eccentric administrative genius"[8]), was it any part of his defined or expected duty. If there is unconstrained choice, it was Oppenheimer's. To say this is not to beg any question about the innocuousness of American politics in the 1940s in contrast with Germany in the 1930s or the Soviet Union in the 1950s; and of course there was some social and political context of wartime, patriotic duty, expectation, and persuasion. It is only to note that whatever the considerations for Oppenheimer in 1942, we can be sure that political pressure (and still less overt coercion) was not among them. By the late 1940s, the story was darker and far more complicated. Oppenheimer among others came to be interrogated on the degree of his enthusiasm for the development of the hydrogen bomb, as a benchmark for loyal anticommunism. In 1942, the picture had been clearer.

৵

In the 1940s, Adorno and Horkheimer argued that the authoritarianism of Nazi Germany was an outcome of enlightenment ideology.[9] It has crossed many minds that the atomic bomb also represents some end point in Western culture, either as a logical result of scientific positivism, or as its reductio ad absurdum, or perhaps just as a full stop to Enlightenment optimism. Oppenheimer himself mused: "The real impact of the creation of the atomic bomb and atomic weapons—to understand that one has to look further back."[10] Although he spent no time on recording reflections at Los Alamos, it was obvious throughout that he understood was he was doing in the widest context.

The first full history of the Manhattan Project was written by a philosopher, David Hawkins, who worked at Oppenheimer's side as an administrator: *Manhattan District History: Project Y: The Los Alamos Project*.[11] Many of the questions raised by Oppenheimer's work have been posed in biographical or historical studies. This book aims to sort out those questions and offer some answers.

To clear the ground, chapter 1, *The Value in a Story*, begins by questioning the point of the whole exercise. How far can a single life at a single time tell us anything general, applicable beyond itself and its own circumstances? What could Oppenheimer represent, beyond himself? Why not think more generally about The Scientist? Or to put the same point in another way, what is the relation between biography and philosophy, or moral philosophy? Or, in still another way, what is the relation between the individual case and the universal rule? Can we have ethics as exemplary narrative or only as moral law? Or, once again, from the other direction: if we could reach no conclusions in moral philosophy about an individual life, what would be the point of the activity? This opening chapter is needed to map out the scope of what can be done: to assess what Kant might have called the possibility of moral philosophy (though Kant's own thinking was at the polar opposite from the style to be followed here). A central aim of the book is to reflect on how we can think directly about an individual life, and to make judgments on it.

Chapter 2, A *Point of Choice?*, looks at choice as a point of appraisal. It is strikingly irrelevant that Oppenheimer's decision to take charge of research on the bomb was preceded by no introspective correspondence or debate, especially in contrast with his worries in 1945 and his still greater concerns later. He chose; he acted. What matters? The choice—or what led him to it? Or the person he was? Or the character he had become? By 1942, he might have said (though he did not, quite) that he had no real choice: this was just how he was, how an American scientist might be expected to act in wartime. But, again, how should a scientist act? And how could that differ from how anybody should act? What is implied by a choice of a way of life, as a scientist? When can a choice be made? Before it is possible to start thinking about responsibility or blame, there must be a need to locate a point of choice or action. This may be less straightforward than it sounds.

Chapter 3, *One Large Fact*, takes the atomic bomb as an extreme challenge to an opposition between fact and value. From the earliest days it was realized that a dichotomy between scientific advisors (for the facts) and political decision-makers (for the values and choices) was going to be strained to the limit by atomic weapons. Even before August 1945 the physicists at Los Alamos insisted on voicing their anxieties to the political and military leadership.[12] In 1962, Groves wrote confidently: "In answer to the question, 'Was the development of the atomic bomb by the United States necessary?' I reply unequivocally, 'Yes.' To the question, "Is atomic energy a force for good or evil?' I can only say, 'As mankind wills it.' "[13] Yet by then the atomic bomb as a specimen of value-neutral fact, independent of human will, must have been deeply implausible. Is this extreme case an exception, or merely the most flagrant example of a schism between fact and value (or science and politics)? Almost no twentieth-century thinker felt comfortable with this schism. To settle convincing reasons for that discomfort is less easy.

Chapter 4, *Curiosity*, asks why we need knowledge. Aristotle asserted boldly but wholly wrongly that "all men by nature desire to know." In reality, a particular sort of curiosity about nature has been specific to particular cultures in particular periods: not, for example, in the period when Augustine condemned unrestrained curiosity as a form of mental greed.[14] Oppenheimer diagnosed the pursuit of knowledge at Los Alamos as an "organic necessity." He said, "If you are a scientist you believe that it is good to find out how the world works."[15] Is this true? Or rather: what could be the alternative? How could you know what not to pursue until you knew about it? In pragmatic terms, how could curiosity be limited in any way that would not do more harm than good? The justification for a pursuit of knowledge is not self-evident or neutral. What a scientist does is only neutral within a context that has come to judge it in that way. The historical context for the development of scientific ideology (in the seventeenth century) is reasonably uncontroversial. We may be able to see how we came to feel as we do. Unfortunately, that does not make it easier to feel otherwise.

Chapter 5 weighs the place of *responsibility*. The atomic bomb is only the most famous case in which intentions and consequences were wildly disconnected. Many of the central figures were drawn to work at Los Alamos because they believed, with the soundest of reasons, that Nazi Germany could and would develop atomic weapons. Yet the first bombs were used on a country where no one thought there could be atomic weapons. This looks like a textbook case of something—but what? The worthlessness of utilitarianism, or maybe its vindication? Or was this the ultimate in what has come to be known as moral luck (rather, ill luck): the best of intentions knocked off course by the unknowability of the future? It is pointless now to think in terms of blame at Los Alamos, though it is hard not to think about responsibility. These issues became sharper with the building of the hydrogen bomb from the late 1940s, then even more obvious with the growth of civilian nuclear power from the 1950s.

The Holocaust of the 1940s or Stalin's purges of the 1930s or the Chinese famine in the 1950s may all seem to call for new moral categories. Yet most of the horrors of the twentieth century are all too repeatable. Something that cannot be repeated or undiscovered is the first creation of atomic weapons. Chapter 6, *Irreversible Change*, considers the asymmetry in cognitive growth—here, the question of whether we get a new moral world from a radically new physics. There is a link with questions of responsibility: Faust. There may be a link with questions about curiosity: Pandora's box. The possibility of total nuclear destruction added a further dimension of irreversibility. As Oppenheimer put it, in one of his most frequently quoted remarks: "In some sort of crude sense which no vulgarity, no humor, no overstatement can quite extinguish, the physicists have known sin; and this is a knowledge which they cannot lose."[16] Even hardened military men who were present for the first atomic test understood this. Brigadier General Thomas F. Farrell wrote in his account: "All seemed to feel that they had been present at the birth of a new age—The Age of Atomic Energy—and felt their profound responsibility to help in guiding into the right channels the tremendous forces which had been unlocked for the first time in history."[17]

Chapter 7, *Purity*, turns to the steps from the theoretical to the practical. Einstein is supposed to have said that he wished he had never framed the theories that made atomic weapons possible. Otto Hahn, who had first reported nuclear fission in the laboratory in 1939, said that he felt "personally responsible for the deaths of hundreds of thousands of people" and contemplated suicide when he heard about Hiroshima.[18] Yet, on the other side, the building of the first bombs was not a matter of pure theory but a collaborative practical effort. Oppenheimer himself liked to say that no new science was needed, that the project was a solely technical challenge. (Though Sakharov described the physics of atomic and thermonuclear explosions as "a genuine theoretician's paradise."[19]) Even if Oppenheimer's diffidence were justifiable, his achievement would remain a supreme example of practical intelligence. In this sense it is quite possible that no one else could have done what he did. But what sort of ability did he display, and what does it imply? In the *Republic* Plato distinguished the expert (with skill: *technê*), who did not interest him in the least, from the ruler (with knowledge: *epistêmê*), who preoccupied him. The distinction is assumed in its modern form by scientists and academics who disparage organization—"administration"—as secondary to creative research. Plato's distinction between practice and theory has been socially and educationally disastrous when taken seriously. (His own record in practical politics, in Sicily, was lamentable.) A great deal has been written about the role of intellectuals. More pertinent questions might be asked on the nature of practical excellence, and on how it is to be appraised. Just as, in chapter 2, we may ask when in a life a point of choice becomes relevant, so chapter 7 looks at where a point of choice or action can be identified in the course of an intricate theoretical-practical project.

The final chapter, The Lessons of History, asks what, if anything, can be learned from Oppenheimer's choice to work at Los Alamos. Indirectly, this goes back to questions on the value of moral reflection and judgment. If philosophy claims to contain anything other than positive knowledge, then what is that? In the twentieth century, wisdom and even understanding as answers provoked only self-conscious embarrassment. It is easy enough to conclude that we are left only with analysis or irony, or, on the other hand, with the summary verdicts of "practical ethics."

Yet a separation between the description or analysis of moral concepts on the one hand and their revision or reform on the other is a false one. There is some point in seeing the frailty of concepts such as choice, responsibility, foresight, judgment. The aim may not be to seek a "philosophical" redrafting of concepts. There is no opposition between understanding and changing the world. It can make a difference to see better, if not perfectly; also, to see the limitations to our vision and judgment. A central aim is not just to think about Oppenheimer, but to reflect on the nature and point of our judgments about him. This must lead to an appraisal of the nature and point of moral reflection: What can we say? What should we say? To what end? What, really, can we learn?

Today, the approach followed in this book could be classed as a study in moral philosophy. In the eighteenth century, before philosophy became an academic specialization, its intentions would have been more familiar: to see a life, or part of a life, clearly and in the right light, and to see ourselves seeing it. Fielding, for example, in his laconic "Exordium" to Amelia in 1751 wrote:

> Life may as properly be called an art as any other; and the great incidents in it are no more to be considered as mere accidents, than the several members of a fine statue, or a noble poem. The critics in all these are not content with seeing any thing to be great, without knowing why and how it came to be so. By examining carefully the several grada-

tions which conduce to bring every model to perfection, we learn truly to know that science in which the model is formed: as histories of this kind, therefore, may properly be called models of HUMAN LIFE; so by observing minutely the several incidents which tend to the catastrophe or completion of the whole, and the minute causes whence those incidents are produced, we shall best be instructed in this most useful of all arts, which I call the ART OF LIFE.

No initial assumptions are made in this study on the nature of philosophy, beyond the fact that it can be characterized as an apparently obsessive pursuit of answers to questions, to questions about questions, and to questions about questions about questions. (Hence, in part, the "reflections" in the subtitle of this book.) Biography can be the archetypal field for the rhetorical shrug of the shoulders: How would it have been different if only . . . ? A philosopher might presume to try to answer a question: Well, how would it have been different . . . ?

CHAPTER ONE

THE VALUE IN A STORY

In 1797, near the end of the *Metaphysics of Morals*, Kant illustrated his views on the use of individual exemplars in the teaching of ethics:

> a teacher will not tell his naughty pupil: take an example from that good (orderly, diligent) boy! For this would only cause him to hate that boy, who puts him in an unfavorable light. A good example (exemplary conduct) should not serve as a model but only as a proof that it is really possible to act in conformity with duty. So it is not comparison with any other human being whatsoever (as he is), but with the *idea* (of humanity), as he ought to be, and so comparison with the law, that must serve as the constant standard of the teacher's instruction.

He had made his point even more provocatively in the *Groundwork of the Metaphysics of Morals* of 1785:

> Nor could one give worse advice to morality than by wanting to derive it from examples. For, every example of it represented to me must itself first be appraised in accordance with principles of morality, as to whether it is also worthy to serve as an original example, that is, as a model; it can by no means authoritatively provide the concept of morality. Even the Holy One of the Gospel must first be compared with our ideal of moral perfection before he is cognized as such. . . . Imitation has no place in matters of morality, and examples serve only for encouragement.[1]

Here is an apparently irremovable obstacle of principle in the way of the project for this book. Biography, naturally, is possible, and may serve as "encouragement." But taking lessons from individual cases is exactly the opposite of what we should do. A single life may illustrate or exemplify a virtue or value. A single choice may exemplify right or wrong. Any kind of judgment must generalize. Any narrative about an individual will be specific. In most interesting cases it will be so specific as to be unique. Oppenheimer himself touched on this in a letter of 1930 where he mentioned a question that had been raised by his brother: "In how far is it possible to formulate ethical rules from which the proper conduct in specific cases may be deduced?" He commented in reply that the question was "too hard to write about, and in my opinion of high importance."[2] He took it no further in writing.

Two conflicting lines of thought need to be confronted. On the one hand, to say anything about actions, decisions, or character must be to describe them, and so to categorize or classify them in some way. From there, following Kant, in short, it seems that we are led toward generalized laws, rules, or principles. Thus, it might be thought more fitting to discuss the role of the scientist in a political context, rather than the complexities of one man's life. Or, more strongly, unless there are worthwhile conclusions on issues such as the role of the scientist, there might seem to be no gain in going into specific detail. On the other hand, Oppenheimer offers a case in which any sort of generalization seems futile. What rule or principle could he exemplify? In a situation when you are asked to lead the research on the first atomic weapons. . . . In a war where your appalling enemy may be developing similar weapons. . . . Hardly common situations. The point comes out still more sharply by asking who "you" might be. Easy to end up asking what would or should be done by a person who could only be Oppenheimer at a time that could only be 1942: so, back to the particulars. Answers to questions about what to do and how to live must be both usefully general and relevantly particular, which seems impossible. Hence, problems not just here but with moral philosophizing more widely. Hence, too, no lessons from history.

This mirrors a tension between biography and philosophy. Even the most schematic or didactic version of a life story—a standard life of a saint, for example—is likely to contain more contingencies than a philosopher may want to handle. Any general conclusions from an individual life may run the risk of simplifying a tangled reality. Interestingly, and paradoxically, the best biographies that have been intended more or less overtly as moral studies can also be the most cautious in pointing to overtly moralistic conclusions. Samuel Johnson's *Life of Mr. Richard Savage*, a saga of violent profligacy and folly, ends calmly: "Those are no proper Judges of his Conduct who have slumber'd away their Time on the Down of Abundance, nor will a wise Man easily presume to say, 'Had I been in *Savage*'s Condition, I should have lived, or written, better than *Savage*.' "[3]

Gitta Sereny's investigation of Franz Stangl, commandant at Treblinka, a catalogue of the most terrible misdeeds that could be imagined, ends with one short page of tentative thoughts about freedom and responsibility which are the author's frank preconceptions as much as deductions from her study.[4]

These are not entirely matters of authorial reticence or reluctance to judge. Letting actions speak for themselves may be more persuasive than open praise or condemnation. And that is not just a question of rhetoric. "Had I been in *Savage*'s Condition . . ." has a point, but only a limited one. Our imagination will only take us so far with Savage; maybe, as Johnson intended, to a point of sympathy, but not as far as to admit that we would ever be in Savage's condition. A reasonable response may be not just be "I would not get myself in that condition" but "Savage should never have put himself in that condition." Sereny's book on Stangl is a classic account of a weak, stupid man sliding from questionable to wholly outrageous work, fortified by an expected range of excuses. Her book is an excellent one partly because the breadth of its message is left open, unlikely to apply to many possible readers, but unfortunately almost as unlikely to apply only to Stangl himself.

It should go without saying that Oppenheimer, too, was, to say the least, an unusual man in an unusual situation between 1942 and 1945. His lawyer at the security hearings in 1954 played this up in his closing peroration:

> You have in Dr. Oppenheimer an extraordinary individual, a very complicated man, a man that takes a great deal of knowing, a gifted man beyond what nature can ordinarily do more than once in a very great while. Like all gifted men, unique, sole, not conventional, not quite like anybody else that ever was or ever will be.

He went on, excusably begging a large question that needs a real answer:

> . . . Does this mean that you should apply different standards
> to him than you would to somebody like me or somebody else
> that is just ordinary? No, I say not. I say that there must not
> be favoritism in this business. You must hew to the line and
> do your duty without favor, without discrimination, if you
> want to use those words.[5]

This may have been sensible advocacy, but its logic is not obvious.
Why should an exceptional man in a unique situation be judged by
the same standards as anyone else? Leaving aside any obvious political
(or religious) bias toward equality, surely everything points in the
opposite direction?

Two questions will help to clear this ground. First: how can
moral reflection be kept particular? (That is: how or where should
it not be generalized?) Second: how or where can the general be
usefully applied to the particular in moral reflection? Both questions
must be faced in dealing with the contingencies of an individual
life. They look similar, but go in differing directions, and not sym-
metrically. In looser terms: how can biography connect with moral
philosophy? And: how can moral philosophy apply to biography?

❧

The first question is, again, rooted in the challenge from Kant. Even
a "unique" person (e.g., a saint or a monster) is a case of something
(saintliness or monstrosity). When Kant wrote (in the second opening quotation to this chapter) "Imitation has no place in matters of
morality" he could have had at least two thoughts in mind. Whenever
you say "act like that" with an individual exemplar, it is always the
"like that," not the individuality, that matters. The exemplar will, by
its nature, have to be a case of something not particular (even a case
of "unparalleled wickedness"). Then—it seems to follow—some general rule will always be assumed or implied. Morality becomes possible
exactly because any particular judgments are of course judgments and
judgments have to include general concepts that are interconnected
in ways not of our individual choosing. This is a strand in the "tran-
sition from popular moral philosophy to metaphysics of morals" that
forms the second part of the *Groundwork of the Metaphysics of Morals*.
Kant thought it clear that "all moral concepts have their seat and
origin [*Sitz und Ursprung*] completely a priori in reason."[6]

Suppose we want to debate a specific choice, such as Oppenheimer's acceptance of the leadership of research at Los Alamos. The questions—judgments—that might arise would include: Was this a good or a right choice? Was it a free choice? What were the alternatives? Then, any imaginable level of debate will require generalities—"choice," "right"—and any level of debate that could be described as moral may require language or concepts that entail some view of morality: What factors were or should have been taken into account? Would they have been the same or different for anyone else relevantly placed in the same situation?

One possibility is to stop this line of thinking from the start, or rather turn it on its head. Iris Murdoch, for example, questioned the orthodox contrast between (on the one hand) concrete individuals knowable—hence judgeable—through abstract concepts (on the other). She was willing to regard at least some moral concepts as "concrete" and, more relevantly here, to regard knowledge of an individual as direct and primary. "It is just the historical, individual, nature of the virtues as actually exemplified which makes it difficult to learn goodness from another person."[7] There is no need to get into any abstract, technical dispute (over knowledge by direct acquaintance against knowledge by description or reference against generality) to see her main idea: that our grasp of individuals and their actions may be firmer than our agreement on a language to describe them, or a set of concepts by which to judge them. This is more interestingly fundamental than Nietzsche's blunt refusal to go down Kant's path:

> No one who judges, "in this case everybody would have to act like this" has yet taken five steps towards self-knowledge. For he would then know that there neither are nor can be actions that are all the same; that every act ever performed was done in an altogether unique and unrepeatable way.[8]

Of course it is true that no actions are the same: exactly as it is impossible to step in the same river twice. Nietzsche himself was robust about the consequences or corollaries. His view would make any legal judgments impossible, in line with his scorn for what he saw as the Kantian reduction of morality to law. But, taken literally, it would also make any use of descriptive language questionable. That might provide support or reinforcement for a view that there can be no description without interpretation. Whether or not all this is a fair version of Nietzsche's position, it is far less defensible than the simpler view of Murdoch. We need no radical skepticism about description, morals, or anything else to feel at least as confident about an individual understanding as about the allegedly underlying logic or principles.

That is a less dogmatic a view than the casuist's assertion that moral knowledge is essentially particular;[9] and it is not quite the point made many times in the long-running difference of opinion between Richard Hare and Thomas Nagel, and echoed in subsequent debates about "moral particularism."[10] Hare wanted to insist that there can be no prelogical (or rather preconceptual) grasp of moral facts. In response, Nagel stressed that specific verdicts are possible without a known or explicit grounding in moral theory. Murdoch's thought is less reassuring than either of these extremes. We may know the individual (or hope we do) but remain uncertain about the concepts or categories through which our knowledge may become manipulable. The next chapter, for example, will ask where we want to apply appraisal to Oppenheimer: to a single choice? a series of choices? a life? a life in science? a personality? Even in picking one single act of choice—a decision to accept a job at Los Alamos—the implied framework of appraisal, consequences, and regret is so indeterminate that there can be no uncontroversial starting-point.

Stronger and clearer thoughts come out from Kant's step toward what he called the moral law. Kant wanted a "pure moral philosophy, completely cleansed of everything that may be only empirical and that belongs to anthropology." To qualify as moral, his laws had to be absolutely necessary and absolutely universal. They had to override absolutely all other considerations. Because of their universality and necessity they would apply not only for humans but for all rational beings. The form of the argument was typically Kantian, resting on the transcendental *unless*. Unless morality was lawlike—that is, universally and impartially binding—it could not exert the force (through duty) that Kant felt it had. Unless it came from a "pure" conceptual source, it could not be universally and impartially binding. The ground of obligation should not be sought "in the nature of the human being or in the circumstances of the world in which he is placed."[11]

Such might be the heart of an objection to a link between biography and philosophy, refigured as a particular case and universal morality. Part of the trouble with it lies in Kant's hyperbole. The justification for his exaggeration of morality into what he called a "system"[12] was not at all self-evident. In the example that he drew from Rousseau for the *Critique of Practical Reason*, someone was pressed, on pain of execution, "to give false testimony against an honorable man." We are asked to recognize only the possibility of a distinction between a sense of duty and a "love of life, however great it may be."[13] Interestingly and relevantly, the example lacks details. To take some banal thoughts, it is not unimaginable that Kant's exemplar might just not grasp *that much* of a sense of duty. Simply, he might not see (still less admire) even the possibility of sacrificing a life for a stranger or for some matter of principle. He might not be an immoralist or an amoralist—just someone whose life or family mattered more than someone else's principles. There seems to be nothing inconsistent about either a limited sense of conscience or a limited understanding of conscience.

There are ways round this. The committed Kantian can go on arguing that only a more general moral rule ("put your family first") can trump a moral rule, and so on. Kant's Abraham should have said: "That I ought not to kill my good son is quite certain. But that you, this apparition, are God—of that I am not certain, and never can be, not even if this voice rings down to me from (visible) heaven."[14] There, moral law took priority over moral or religious intuition. (Kierkegaard drew diametrically opposite conclusions at great length from the same example in *Fear and Trembling.*)

A far greater problem arises from the nature of the move to "law" understood in terms of universality and necessity. The real difficulty is neither that the purity of morality is itself a value, in a question-begging way (as Bernard Williams suggested[15]), nor that a recourse to law is to wash out the morals in morality (as Nietzsche thought). To mistrust a reliance on an individual example because the moral law must be abstract—"pure"—and general is to abandon one form of narrative, which has its feet on the ground, in favor of another, which does not. Kant's extensive use of legal and political metaphor was rooted in an evidently partial understanding of law. To experience a sense of duty, for example, is to understand compulsion (dramatized into necessitation) and some notion of fairness (dramatized into universality). His story was that "pure reason, *practical of itself*, is . . . immediately lawgiving. The will is thought as independent of empirical conditions and hence, as pure will, as determined *by the mere form of law.*" Or again: "Every concept of duty involves objective constraint through a law"—a thought followed by a torrent of legal imagery:

the internal *imputation* of a *deed*, as a case falling under a law, belongs to the *faculty of judgment*. . . . Upon it follows the conclusion of *reason* (the verdict), that is, the connecting of the rightful result with the action (condemnation or acquittal). All this takes place before a *tribunal*, which, as a moral person giving effect to the law, is called a *court*.—Consciousness of an *internal court* in the human being . . . is *conscience*.[16]

The appeal to legal metaphor was supposed to be to a set of concepts that would be intelligible and, presumably, acceptable to Kant's enlightened readers. Law was assumed to be fair and general in its nature. A fine thought from the end of the eighteenth century, but unfortunately not one to be taken for granted, and still less to bear so much theoretical weight. The medieval English legal dictum "the king shall be under God and the law" was not a description or analysis of a concept of law but, at least, a declaration of a wish to contain royal power. Its normativity came from baronial force, not logic. The vindication for Kant's elaborate imagery of debates in the tribunal of reason may be portrayed positively as "recursive" rather than circular, tied constructively to a central value of autonomy. Yet we can still ask why a tribunal or debate *has* to be conducted according to rules of Enlightenment impartiality. There may be a pragmatic answer. As Onora O'Neill puts it, "Debate cannot survive the adoption of principles destroying debate."[17] But why should it survive in that way? Why should that matter?

This is all unpalatably abstract. There is a concrete link with the quotation from Oppenheimer's lawyer a few pages back. In the 1954 tribunal he asked, again: "Does this mean that you should apply different standards to him than you would to somebody like me or somebody else that is just ordinary?" And his own reply was: "No, I say not. I say that there must not be favoritism in this business." In what was, literally, a legal context, that may have been appropriate. There may have been "standards" against which it may have been necessary to appraise Oppenheimer's actions: Kant's "objective constraint." In an American legal context such standards could only be represented as impartial and impersonal. Was this not the only way in which Oppenheimer should be judged? One possible response might be to point to his uniqueness as a man and to the unrepeatability of the situations in which he was placed in the 1940s. His lawyer did try this, but only as a rhetorical gesture, no doubt mindful that Napoleonic exceptionalism might not impress his audience. Another response might be to underline the difference between the actual practice of justice (in the McCarthyite fever of 1954) and ideal (or even acceptable) standards of judgment. That would be an appeal to morality or politics behind law, bringing out a difference between how the law should be and how it was in reality.

This specific case shows what is not helpful about a Kantian approach. If an individual is to be judged, it should be according to law-like principles. But whose law-like principles, and where? And why, for that matter, be so keen on judgment at all? For Kant, such questions would be absurd. The moral law must be absolute, for all rational beings. Crucially, the standards for the law can come from nothing but itself, not—particularly not—from human or divine endorsement. Kant might take the view that law would not be law if it were not like this. The world might be a better place if he were right. Unfortunately, there is no reason to take his view as anything but an enlightened recommendation.

Biography can bring something to philosophy because the value or sense in a story lies at least as plausibly in the individual story itself as in some more general narrative of principles and law. Which is to say that philosophical ambitions toward abstraction or generality must be treated with some care.

✌❧

In another direction, though, what can the philosopher bring to a life story? Why not leave it to the biographer or historian? One reply might be that this kind of demarcation is pointless. Any distinctiveness might just as well be a matter of focus and emphasis. Philosophers have tried occasionally to understand their own lives through autobiography, and sometimes to characterize that kind of understanding.[18] There is no need to stake out some exclusively philosophical perspective. This book, for example, does not try to portray the whole of Oppenheimer's life or to consider anything in it after 1945. Wittgenstein compared philosophy to a slow bicycle race. "This is how philosophers should salute each other: 'Take your time!' "[19] A philosopher does not find it odd to slow the pace of inquiry to a degree that the most minute historian would find intolerable. Even more narrowly, this is a study of only one choice, or series of choices, that Oppenheimer made, together with their context. Perhaps characteristically for philosophy, it reflects not just on

Oppenheimer, but on ourselves reflecting on him. Few of the relevant facts are in doubt. The real problem is what to make of them. A large part of the interest is that we do not know what apparatus to use—what attitudes or forms of judgment might be appropriate. Philosophy often requires some reflection on itself just as moral judgment always reflects something on the nature of morality, while useful history need not contain any implications for historiography.

A good deal was written about clarity during the heyday of analytic philosophy in the middle of the last century, as though philosophers had some claim to superior or more precise vision. A less charged ambition could be to sort out different issues and think about them one at a time. This is what is attempted in the chapters of this book. Insofar as Oppenheimer can be seen as representative, he was surely representative of many different questions or themes: the location of choice in a life, the place for responsibility, the relation between scientific theory and action, and so on. This is so even though his fame rests mainly on one single achievement. He, and it, had many dimensions. Most obviously, we can wonder how far a scientific urge toward inquiry can be reconciled with a need to make decisions at a time when their full consequences cannot be known. To draw questions apart and to deal with them separately is not to suggest that they can be autonomous. It is just a step toward any sort of useful progress. But that assertion can be vindicated only by some illuminating results.

CHAPTER TWO

A POINT OF CHOICE?

La chose la plus importante à toute la vie est le choix du métier: le hasard en dispose.

—Pascal, *Pensées*

Oppenheimer was relatively late in joining American research leading toward the atomic bomb. The preliminaries had been under way since 1939. He went to his first conference in October 1941 and took over fast neutron research at Berkeley in January 1942. The appointment of Leslie Groves as military head of the Manhattan Project in September 1942 moved the work into a dramatically practical phase. Groves made rapid intuitive decisions. Research was to be centralized. Oppenheimer was to lead it. There is no record of hesitation between Groves and Oppenheimer. Groves had difficulties in convincing his superiors that Oppenheimer, despite his complete absence of organizational experience and doubtful political contacts, was the person for the job. Nevertheless, Groves chose Oppenheimer and together they selected Los Alamos as the site for the project during November 1942. Oppenheimer began to recruit physicists. From March 1943 until the summer of 1945, his life was based at Los Alamos.

At the time he said almost nothing about his thoughts or motives. In February 1943, he wrote to I. I. Rabi, who was unwilling to join the project:

I think if I believed with you that this project was "the culmination of three centuries of physics," I should take a different stand. To me it is primarily the development in time of war of

a military weapon of some consequence. I do not think that the
Nazis allow us the option of carrying out that development.[1]

Oppenheimer, like most of the physicists who began with the
project in 1943 (including many exiles from Germany and central
Europe), believed, with some reason, that atomic research was advancing in Germany. For them, that was justification enough.

Oppenheimer's point of choice looks too obvious to be worth
much debate. He was asked whether he wanted to be in charge of
atomic research. He chose to accept. When the lack of progress in
German atomic research became evident in 1944, followed by the
defeat of Germany in 1945, he did not waver in his commitment to
the project. He chose to maintain his original decision.

Equally clearly, it seems that we can ask whether his choice was
the right one. After all, it was a plain matter of yes or no. Some
physicists, including Rabi, chose not to participate directly at first,
with no loss to their standing. What could be more straightforward?
This would have been how Oppenheimer saw it himself. At the time,
he was not at all inclined to portray himself as a victim of fate,
unlucky enough to be the right man destined to fill a tragic role. He
ruminated later on his motives, not always consistently, but there is
no useful record of what he was thinking from 1942 to 1945. This
does not matter. In fact, it makes things simpler. Some have speculated negatively on what lay behind his actions. Robert Jungk implied
that Oppenheimer felt a failure in comparison with his scientific friends
and that the atomic bomb "offered an opportunity to accomplish
something exceptional in quite another direction." There is no evidence to support this. Teller took a more critical line. Oppenheimer's
belief, he suggested, was that the bomb project would enhance the
lowly status of physicists.[2] In any event, retrospective psychologizing
looks wholly beside the point. Personal feelings seem out of proportion with a practical step of such magnitude.

Yet we may still want to ask (what sounds like one naïve question underlying this book): How could someone *like him* do something
like that? One factual answer of course is: Quite easily, since we know
that he showed no hesitation. But that answer, like the question, does
not get us far. If Oppenheimer's motives had been more explicit, or
if he had left an unequivocal record ("I'll do this to leave my mark on
history—end the war—serve my country—improve my career—save
Europe from Hitler . . .") then he might have been a less interesting

man, but the discussion in this book would have to be much the same. We would want to inquire about the rightness of his choice regardless of his motives, or his accuracy in identifying them. There might arise the separate point that a right or wrong choice can derive from a sound or defective motive; but that is hardly new, and it would add nothing important.

But is it all so clear? A definite point of choice, where appraisal or judgment clearly must apply, however uncertainly? It is easy to think in terms of chicken-or-egg alternatives. In one direction, any decision, if it is not to be arbitrary, has to be the outcome of background, education, character, and (no doubt) biology. In another, a decision feels different from a forecast or prediction. "What shall I do next?" feels radically different from "What am I going to do next?" These alternatives can branch out into deadlocks between determinism and freedom, between good and right, or between character and action.

In Oppenheimer's case there was, on the one hand, the clearest possible point of decision. He could have refused Groves's overtures in 1942 or he could have taken a lesser part in the Manhattan Project. On the other hand, in the words of a letter he wrote to his brother in 1930, "The reason why a bad philosophy leads to such hell is that it is what you think and want and treasure and foster in times of preparation that determines what you do in the pinch, and that it takes an error to father a sin."[3] The clear decision in 1942 was taken by a particular physicist in his late thirties, from New York, recently married, experienced in nuclear theory and research, fond of deserts, poetry, philosophy. In a way, such background seems absurdly irrelevant. After all, it was the outcome of the decision—a momentous one—that mattered, not the man who took it, and certainly not his thoughts or feelings. In another way, if there are questions about responsibility (to be discussed in chapter 5), then it is reasonable to ask how or when any responsibility bore on Oppenheimer, and at what point, rather than on anyone else connected with the project. This is not simple, either in factual terms or in principle. Factually, there is a good case that his contribution was unique. This is not to say that no one else would or could have built the bomb. It is to say that no one else might have built it to be used when it was—a painfully relevant proviso. That should not be too historically controversial to be accepted for the sake of argument. ("Los

Alamos was Oppenheimer's time of glory," said Hans Bethe much later, "and nobody else could have done it."[4]) The issue of principle follows immediately. This was not an action taken by the holder of a particular office, but a decision by a specific man who went on to succeed in a job where others might not have.

Here the important point is easy to miss. It may seem attractive to ask of any present or future choice how someone else might act in the same position. This—again—is part of the appeal of Kantian thinking. "What should I do?" can always be related to "What should someone relevantly similar in a relevantly similar position do?" Although there are obvious difficulties, this seems at least plausible. It has the appearance of a helpful decision technique. But it unravels in looking at the past. "What should he have done?" cannot be detached from how things turned out.

The role of time is essential. The important effect of aftersight is neither a matter of reckoning consequences nor an aspect of what has come to be known as moral luck. If German atomic bombs had been developed successfully and then used to devastate Europe, the reputation of Heisenberg would be even worse than it is. Even as it was, purely in terms of consequences there is actually some case to blame him for Hiroshima and Nagasaki. Much of the impetus behind research came from the fact that many of the physicists at Los Alamos were all too aware that someone of his ability and pertinacity was connected with Nazi bomb development. As Oppenheimer said in 1954, "We had information in those days of German activity in the field of nuclear fission. We were aware of what it might mean if they beat us to the draw in the development of atomic bombs."[5]

One of Heisenberg's varied rationalizations after 1945 was that German scientists had not tried hard to build an atomic bomb, either because of their delicate consciences or because of a decision taken in 1942 by Albert Speer (either fortunately or not, depending on the audience). Presumably Heisenberg was aware of some spectrum of discredit between not trying hard to build a bomb for Hitler, not being pressed to build it, trying and not succeeding, and (the most likely possibility) making a rash miscalculation that a bomb would be impracticable. Even if a German bomb had been *nearly* ready in 1945 as a result of Heisenberg's work, his subsequent reputation might have been different: wicked rather than merely shoddy.[6] The answer to the question: What should he have done? is given without too much obscurity by the example of German scientists who found ways not to work with him.

The point of such a negative parallel is not merely that Oppenheimer has to be seen as someone who had the moral luck (or ill luck) to be head of a project that succeeded, with large consequences. Although that is true, it is just as true that he might be viewed differently if the test bomb at Alamogordo had failed to go off. As Nagel put it, "We judge people for what they actually do or fail to do, not just for what they would have done if circumstances had been different."[7]

Consequence- or duty-based moral theories may seem helpful in offering rules or procedures to anyone in deciding what to do next, but they share a common failing that can be brought out in reflecting on the past rather than the future. The connection between a person, an action, and its consequences is never accidental in retrospect. The alleged problem of moral luck should bring this out. Richard Rorty speculated on an imaginary Heidegger who married a Jewish student and left Germany for the United States in the early 1930s, to return only after 1945. "He had the good luck to have been unable to have become a Nazi, and so to have had less occasion for cowardice or hypocrisy."[8] Rorty's aim was to argue the contingency of the links between Heidegger's writing and his actual life. The life might be imagined to be radically different, while the works might not differ so much. This was meant to be a case against the idea of an "essential Heidegger." As a persuasive literary device, such counterfactual history may be entertaining. As argument, its merit is less clear. The form of the argument is that we can tell a story about a recognizable Heidegger without some of his actions, so the person and these actions are contingently related. This is logic that needs to include time. Different senses of possibility are at work. Yesterday it was possible for me to go to London, but I stayed in Cambridge. Going to London was a possible choice for me yesterday. Today it is not possible in the same sense that I might have been in London yesterday. In fact it is not possible at all that the person I am today was in London yesterday.[9] That would have to be—literally, not figuratively—someone else. The fiction that past actions might be counterfactually detachable is misleading. This is because in some important sense in choosing what to do next I am also choosing who I shall be next: a person who has taken certain decisions or not. Superficially, the contingency that can be insinuated between me and my actions—I might not have done them—is more plausible than a contingency between my past and present selves. A 1940s existentialist might insist on my capacity to remake myself at any moment: to make wild choices that will turn me into a different person. If that has any relevance for the future, it unravels when applied to the past.

This may be so even with a single action. Conrad's Lord Jim was ruined by one catastrophic moment of weakness when he was a young man. His story consists of what happens to him afterward: the person he became as a result. If we learn of how he came to make his mistake, it is not through anything the author tells us directly. Anyway, this is comparatively unimportant. What matters is what did happen, not what led to it, or what might have happened. It was Jim's bad luck that his private weakness turned into a public disgrace. He could not have known or predicted this. Often, an unknowable amount of what happens may be beyond the knowledge or control of someone's making a decision. That is often cited as a factor against utilitarian (or generally consequentialist) moral theorizing. Its effects are wider. In acting as a coward, Jim became a person who had been a coward. Plainly, one point of the story is that he cannot detach his past act of cowardice, even as a possibility, from his personality (however hard he tries). If he had acted otherwise, he would not have been the person he was, but someone else.

Thus, there is an asymmetry between the interesting but unanswerable question of how Oppenheimer may have decided what to do in 1942 and the present question of how he is seen today: between his "What shall I do now?" and our "What should he have done then?" An attempt to objectify the first question—to turn it, as far as possible, into something like the second question—is flawed in both directions. In one direction, there is something badly wrong about turning his decision about what to do in 1942 into an impersonal judgment. In the other, an impersonal verdict is of no relevance to his decision. In both, the problem is that he, not someone else, and certainly not anyone in general, was different as a result of the decision. This point has nothing to do with an inability to foresee the future when Oppenheimer made his decision, and still less to do with a contrast between internal and external perspectives. It is to do with time and identity.

The existentialist prospect of a wholly different future is obviously not impossible. Real life, as well as literature, is full of characters whose subsequent lives have been redirected by single decisions, bizarre or otherwise. The dubious inference is from the banal thought that a life can be wholly changed to the conclusion that it is a different life. Again, this is plain from the past. I can't decide now to be "a different person" in the future because then my past—who I am now—can't be disowned. (Bernard Williams: "There is an authority exercised by what one has done."[10])

This is the trouble in an appeal from "What should I do?" to "What should someone relevantly similar in a relevantly similar position do?" There is an excellent factual case that few people have been relevantly similar to Oppenheimer and that none have been in a position relevantly similar to his in 1942. Those historical points are only symptomatic of the underlying matter of principle. No one else was ever going to be Oppenheimer, with his past life and choices. So no one else could ever be in anything like a relevantly similar position.

But so what? This looks like a slippery slope toward an unacceptable conclusion. We start reasonably enough by asking whether we are thinking about a man or his actions, and then go through some arguments along the lines that actions are only doubtfully detachable from agents. Does it follow then that there can be no valuable discussion of actions without consideration of who performed them? That sounds absurd and irresponsible. Here is an action of the largest practical consequence: the development of an atomic bomb. Why should it matter whether one physicist or another was in charge? (Would they have cared in Hiroshima?) One reply might be to agree, but to point out that this is not what is being discussed. The place for individual responsibility in a large project that was—perhaps—going to proceed anyway is a theme for chapters 5 and 7. For now the point is more personal: Oppenheimer's role in the project—not the final use of the bomb, but its first steps. At that stage, questions about *his* part are not irrelevant. If it is worth asking how an individual should act, then it seems necessary first to work out how to see and identify actions. Again, for what, exactly, is Oppenheimer praised or blamed or, more neutrally, judged?

For his successful achievement? Or the first steps toward it? We can ask: should he have started on this? But how meaningful is that? If Oppenheimer had said no to Groves in 1942, he would have become a different person, not the famous Oppenheimer of the Manhattan Project. In a less trite sense, if he had said no to Groves he would already have been a different person. The interest here is obscured by the exaggerations of past theorizing. Those who want to make a minimal case for free will can stress that there was certainly a time when Oppenheimer could have refused Groves's offer. Thus, there would be an identifiable point of choice at which his, and our, verdict could focus. At the other extreme, it is possible to imagine an insistence that the person who existed in 1942 could not have chosen otherwise, given his character, background, and so on. Yet the difficult issue is surely not one of freedom but of identity. The sense of possibility in which philosophers can debate whether someone *could* have acted otherwise is a diversion from the point of real interest.

One view—usually ascribed to Kant—is that issues of freedom and of identity are interrelated. In regarding myself as a person with a choice, I am identifying myself as a free, rational agent. In ascribing freedom to myself, I may have to see myself as an autonomous human agent rather than, for example, someone obeying orders or merely following a set of professional rules. A purist will want to say: this person has a choice at any moment, or a conscience. Even at the moment of feeling "I have no choice in this," an individual may know that there is, in some theoretical sense, a choice. How important is this? To choose to act *as* an American physicist sounds as though it is to opt out of some wider reckoning. How should a physicist act? How should an American act? How should a citizen act in time of war? There may be historical reasons to insist that such questions must always be subordinated to an apparently wider question: How should a human being act? Yet a real, concrete case forces us to ask about a real person with a real history: what could or should someone have done in the situation he or she was in? And—once again—what situation, and when? Goaded by cross-examination at the 1954 hearing, Oppenheimer said with characteristic sharpness, "I did my job which was the job I was supposed to do. I was not in a policy-making position at Los Alamos. I would have done anything that I was asked to do, including making the bombs in a different shape, if I had thought it was technically feasible."[11]

In an Aristotelian ethic of virtues, a choice of career might be an archetypal ethical choice. (No one could feel much sympathy for someone who volunteers for a job as a guard in a concentration camp and then suffers from scruples about how brutally to act. A person who has taken a job as a village police officer in a peaceful democracy might arouse some sympathy if the society turns into a violent dictatorship.) One of the ways why Oppenheimer's life is instructive is that a choice of physics as a career in the early 1920s contained no intimations of difficult choices in the future. Anyone deciding to take up nuclear physics since the 1950s has been aware of a need to reflect on the palatability of likely future sources of work and money, as well as possible limits to the free publication of research. In comparison, the 1920s and 1930s were an age of innocence. At the start of Oppenheimer's career, a choice of fundamental physics contained no more moral or ethical implications than a choice of botany or paleontology. His position by 1942 has parallels among scientists who started impeccably theoretical careers in genetics or molecular biology in the 1960s to run into starkly practical questions of power and corporate greed by the end of the century. This shows a paradox, if not a contradiction, in a supposed ethic of virtues. It is arguable that Oppenheimer in 1942 acted just as an American physicist should act, as an American physicist. Yet, obviously, he did not choose to be an American and he did not choose to be a physicist whose work would be relevant to the building of atomic bombs, though this is what he became. Any identifiable point of appraisal seems blurred.

Part of the trouble may stem from the pervasive appeal of legal metaphors. It is tempting to think of *judging* a person's action, where the act is the focus of judgment and the character of the agent is taken into account as mitigation or, more loosely, background. Naturally, there may be good reasons for this. If Oppenheimer had not accepted his work with the bomb, or if it had not succeeded, we would not be thinking about him as we do. But there are also reasons to resist a narrowing of appraisal to a legal model. It may beg the most interesting questions.

By way of contrast to a legal perspective, Stoic moralists liked animal imagery. They might start from a comparison between a welltrained dog and the unthinking reflexes of a well-trained athlete and slide on to the moral reflexes of a well-educated person. That sounds wholly unhelpful, as though moral decision-making can be absorbed or reduced into automism—Pascal's *abêtissement*—and education reduced to training. One Stoic thought was not just that it is important to be the sort of character who knows what to do without calculation, but that calculation in itself reveals the wrong sort of character. For example, Epictetus:

Agrippinus, when Florus was considering whether he should
go to Nero's shows, so as to perform some part in them himself, said to him, "Go."—"So why do you not go yourself?"
said Florus. "Because," replied Agrippinus, "I do not even
consider doing so." For as soon as a person even considers
such questions, comparing and calculating the values of external things, he draws close to those who have lost all sense of
their proper character.[12]

The significance is not in the cultivation of gentlemanly Roman
sang froid but in the relation between character and action. The
successors to Kant and Sartre may be inclined to suspect heteronomy
or inauthenticity. The unfairness in such a diagnosis can be seen from
an asymmetry with actions that may be held to be praiseworthy.
Vladimir Bukovsky, who spent twelve years in Soviet prison camps
and psychiatric hospitals, wrote in his memoirs of his first steps on a
path toward dissent at the age of ten. He resigned as chairman of the
Young Pioneers in his class over a slight to a classmate. "I realized I
couldn't play this idiotic role any longer. I resigned. They tried talking me round, upbraided me, censured me, but I stuck to my guns. I
didn't explain the reason for my resignation—I don't think I could
have done so." Bukovsky's action is seen as a matter of conscience,
though, as he says, it was inexplicable even to himself and almost
automatic. It was certainly disinterested. (" 'Watch out,' said my friends,
'you'll find it harder to get into the university.' "[13]) Why should an
action that strikes us as positive impress us as authentic or autonomous when we think in opposite terms about actions that seem blame-
worthy or questionable? In countless cases, moral heroes assure us that
they had no choice but to act as they did. The impression of heroism
is reinforced rather than undermined. Why?

The emphasis for the moral hero may be: *I* had no choice or *I*
saw no alternatives (*ich kann nicht anders*).[14] A purist will see this as
a mere figure of speech. (A cynic may see it as vanity.) If you have
no choice and no alternatives, then your actions should be constrained:
no room for heroism or any other sort of appraisal. But that
simplification surely misses the sense of the emphasis. Not: *I* had no
choice but others (less heroically) would have had a choice; nor: *I* saw
no alternatives but others would have seen some. Instead: as I am, I
never considered acting otherwise. This should be significant beyond
the narrow field of moral heroism, to negative or morally neutral

actions as well as to positive ones. Oppenheimer wrote to Rabi, "I do not think that the Nazis allow us the option." This could not mean "we had no choice" in either a literal sense or in some sense that might interest a philosopher preoccupied with the theory of free will. What it does mean requires a good deal of thought.

The Stoic project (suggested by Epictetus in the previous quotation) may have been to turn yourself into the sort of person who can never even consider a base action. One prosaic interpretation is that you can alter or develop your character, but, once you have it, your real choices are constrained. Then you do what you should, as you are. One trouble with this is circularity. You may never discover that you are (for example) the sort of character who would not betray your friends under torture. You may hope that you are, or may fortify your resolution in advance, but the only test of that sort of character may be the torture itself. Further, although we can understand the notion of completely unreflective heroic actions, it is not clear why they should be regarded as particularly admirable. The hero who dives into an icy river to rescue a child without a second's thought is only a second more admirable than someone who reflects for an instant on the consequences before diving in. (What about the hero who dives in the river without a second's thought and then ends up drowned himself, in comparison with someone who reflects for a second on the consequences and prefers to stay alive?) Whatever we think about such examples, it is very unclear why the extent of reflection should be relevant. It is a mistake to think that acting without reflection—even on the worthiest impulses—covers the important part of what may be meant by having no choice in a sense that matters. Homeric heroes frequently reflected at length on their fates while knowing at the same time what they were going to do and what was going to happen to them.

The relevant factor in "I never considered acting otherwise" cannot be either a presence or absence of conscious reflection, or a repudiation of autonomy. An underlying metaphor could be more one of authorship than legal agency: not a crime that someone else might have committed, but a book that no one else could have written. The change of imagery from legalistic to literary need not imply that morality is reduced to aesthetics; though, in the opposite perspective, the extensive use of legal imagery in moral philosophy may indeed have significant implications. The courtroom separation of act from agent is meant to invite questions about how others might have acted or how a similar deed might have been performed by others. That approach may be necessary for a judicial verdict. There is little point, on the other hand, in asking whether an author might have written a wholly different book, and almost no point in asking whether a particular book might have been written by a different author.

This may seem far-fetched, distasteful language to apply to the atomic bomb. Yet in resorting to the jargon of the courts—judgment, verdicts, impartiality, detachment—we may be making it harder for ourselves to resolve the most troublesome points. Authorship offers one different perspective. More commonly used, but evidently less neutral, is the prelegal language of stigma and pollution, the Greek *miasma*.[15] Mere association with a deed, however involuntary or "unlucky," may carry a taint that has nothing to do with a point of "responsible" choice or agency. Hannah Arendt wrote of Nuremberg and other war crimes trials: "the judges in all these trials really passed judgment solely on the basis of the monstrous deeds. In other words, they judged freely, as it were, and did not really lean on the standards and legal precedents with which they more or less convincingly sought to justify their decisions."[16]

Adam Smith's account of "the influence of fortune upon the sentiments of mankind, with regard to the merit or demerit of actions" peers into these historical shadows more cannily than later work on moral luck. Smith was entirely aware that we *should* respect the "just and equitable maxim, That those events which did not depend upon our conduct, ought not to diminish the esteem which is due to us." He distinguished between the light in which an agent "at present appears" and "that in which he ought to appear," arguing that we *ought* to regularize our sentiments. He offered an anthropological explanation for our irregularity:

> It is . . . of considerable importance, that the evil which is done without design should be regarded as a misfortune to the doer as well as to the sufferer. Man is thereby taught to reverence the happiness of his brethren, to tremble lest he should, even unknowingly, do any thing that can hurt them, and to dread that animal resentment which, he feels, is ready to burst out against him, if he should, without design, be the unhappy instrument of their calamity.

And he went on to trace some history in "the ancient heathen religion."[17] Some of his diagnosis was surely right. Feelings of remorse or pity, which must have something to do with some older ethical frame-work, undoubtedly do attach to deeds in which responsibility plays no real part. From the same line of thinking, it might seem that the consequences of Oppenheimer's "choice" that led him to the bomb were so momentous that quibbling over a specific point of decision is just frivolous. In readily intelligible terms, there is no way of escaping his association with the outcome. So identification of some clear locus of responsibility is beside the point.

This may be understandable but there are two elements of confu-sion. First, more generally, the cloud of horror that hangs over the use of the first atomic bombs seems to obscure any fine shades of discrimi-nation. Maybe so, but we can only try. Second, if Adam Smith were right, there would be very little more to say. Some primitive ethic might well condemn anyone connected with a terrible deed, whatever the degree of culpability or choice. It might be true that some recollec-tion of atavistic pollution still lingers in our minds. But, as Smith said, it is also true that we can ask whether we ought to feel like this.

A model of authorship may be less dramatic but could be more valuable. It is often remarked that the most trivial biographical and personal details about writers, painters, or composers are published and read with interest, whereas even the most important scientists may remain comparatively unknown. It is possible to practice a sci-ence at the highest level while knowing nothing of its history or its past heroes. There is no mystery here. Plainly, the underlying feeling is that a scientific theory or discovery is autonomous in that it may not matter who produced it. No one needs to know, and the knowl-edge makes no difference to its worth. Further, it might have been produced in a different way or at a different time by someone else.

Chapter 7 will look at the difference between theoretical and practical science. One initial thought might be that the theory be-hind the making of the first atomic bombs could have been developed in other ways by other research teams, but the practical development took place when and how it did, under the leadership of Oppenheimer. It is also arguable—and this will be pursued later—that restraint in the theoretical growth in the sciences is a good deal less feasible that restraint in practical, applied developments. Evidently, it is hard to undiscover theoretical discoveries once they have been made, while it may be easy not to put them into practical effect. So there is a case to ascribe authorship of the bombs to Oppenheimer in some personal sense, not applicable to a theoretical invention or discovery.

There is one corollary from this shift of metaphors. "If I don't do this, then someone else (worse) will" has always been seen as a disastrous argument. (Why not sell heroin? Someone will.) Hans Bethe said in 1968 of the H-bomb project: "If I didn't work on the bomb somebody else would—and I had the thought if I were around Los Alamos I might still be a force for disarmament. So I agreed to join in developing the H-bomb."[18] Yet on the other hand, a strict insistence on individual responsibility does seem beside the point where something may indeed happen anyway, somehow. In fact this is entirely how the argument gets its persuasiveness. If an action can be wholly detachable from its agent—anyone could (and may) do it— then the next step is the thought that the identity of the agent is not that significant, especially if it can be seen as unavoidable anyway. This might be the case, for example, in some branches of interesting but questionable research. It might sound plausible (if only to the apologist) to take a job researching into chemical warfare on the grounds that other candidates might be less scrupulous. In 1942, it was true that if Oppenheimer had declined to work on the bomb, then someone else would have been invited; though it is also true that no other candidates were in sight.

The difficulty here is not helped by escalation to extremes. It is easy to stress that a free agent has the ability to decide to act or not at any point. This may be useful as a stipulative definition of a *free agent*, but it only has a practical use if that abstract character can be identified in reality. To regard any divergences from the pure case as evasions or excuses is to beg the question. When Oppenheimer was asked to take charge of research on the atomic bomb, of course he "could" have refused. But it is not merely equivocating apologetics to say that the point of choice was not so simple. If obligation is supposed to be universalizable—he *ought to* means that anyone positioned identically ought to—then it is doubtful whether he could be said to have been obliged to choose one way or another (since no one else could have been positioned identically). In fact, if the universality of obligation is taken seriously, it suggests that someone in a truly unique predicament would indeed have no choice, exactly reflecting the vague thought: *I* could not do otherwise, or: *I* had no alternative. That vague thought confirms the suspicion that it is not anyone but *me* who has to choose, as *I* am. In 1942, it was not anyone who was asked to take on the atomic bomb, but a specific person with a specific history and background, where the alternative choices were entirely unclear.

A first reaction might be that here must be some dilution of responsibility, as in: I had no choice—at the worst: I was only obeying orders. A better interpretation could be the opposite, as in: I had no choice, no one else could do it. A negative view of autonomy might stress a lack of outside influence. A positive view might stress the *acceptance* of responsibility as much as the significance of choice.

These first two chapters have been abstract and methodological. Their point can be put in simple Platonic terms: one of *seeing* the subject properly. There are obvious tensions between a view of Oppenheimer as a concrete individual and a grasp of the general questions that may be raised by his life. There are similar tensions between any discussion of a single crucial step that he took and a wider view of his biography. It is not clear in either case that a commonsense compromise is available or productive.

Abstraction does make discussion easier, but it may also be a form of evasion. To insist that moral debate must be personal may be to suggest that it must have an aim—or at least a context. It does not exist in the abstract, for its own sake. This may be a key to the awkward asymmetries between present choice and future judgment. This will come up again in chapter 5, in asking about our position in making a judgment on decisions in 1942.

CHAPTER THREE

ONE LARGE FACT

In his farewell speech to the Association of Los Alamos Scientists on November 2, 1945, Oppenheimer said:

> If you are a scientist you believe that it is good to find out how the world works; that it is good to find out what the realities are; that it is good to turn over to mankind at large the greatest possible power to control the world and to deal with it according to its lights and values.[1]

The model he had in mind was one that would have been familiar to all his listeners. The scientist finds out the realities. Humanity at large decides what to do, according to its lights and values. In the United States of the 1940s, humanity's will was expressed through the constitutionally elected government and its appointed officials. Years later, Edward Teller wrote of Oppenheimer in 1945, of the discussions before Hiroshima,

> that he thought it improper for a scientist to use his prestige as a platform for political pronouncements. He conveyed to me in glowing terms the deep concern, thoroughness, and wisdom with which these questions were being handled in Washington. Our fate was in the hands of the best, the most conscientious men of our nation.[2]

Whatever one makes of this retrospective sarcasm, the distinction between scientists and government was supposed to be a clear one, grounded in a clear division between facts and values.

Even by 1945, though, things were not so simple in practice. Oppenheimer himself was already immersed in scientific advisory and control committees. He remained at the heart of government decision-making until his exclusion in 1954. Many in his audience at Los Alamos in 1945 would not have accepted the suggestion in his words of a separation between realities and values, or the implied subordination of science to politics. The scientists' movement in America (anatomized excellently by Alice Kimball Smith in A Peril and a Hope) had been active through the final stages of the Manhattan Project. One of its main demands was for a greater voice for atomic scientists in the formation of government policy. But there seems to have been no doubt that final decisions on the use of atomic weapons should be political, not scientific. Oppenheimer, with Compton, Lawrence, and Fermi, signed a set of "Recommendations on the Immediate Use of Nuclear Weapons" in June 1945 that ended:

> It is true that we are among the few citizens who have had occasion to give thoughtful consideration to these problems during the past few years. We have, however, no claim to special competence in solving the political, social, and military problems which are presented by the advent of atomic power.[3]

This was certainly the case at a much earlier stage in the project. The decision to commit huge resources to practical research and development was taken by politicians—ultimately by Roosevelt. Without the money (the whole program cost two billion dollars) and without the political will, there would have been no bombs. Yet equally, without the physicists there would have been no bombs. Possibly without Oppenheimer there would have been no bomb by July 1945. Any inevitability in the project is an illusion.

How far can a separation be sustained between the "realities" of the bomb and the questions about "values" that arise from its development? That looks like a straightforward question about a separation between fact and value. Maybe it is; but on the other hand the atomic bomb itself seems to be an affront to a separation between fact and value. If "facts" are supposed to be value-free, then the atomic bomb seems more than anomalous.

More important, in a political way, how does a contrast between facts and values match up with a distinction between science and politics? What sort of decision-making is appropriate where extremely specialized knowledge may be necessary? In 1950, a disillusioned Oppenheimer wrote:

> Is there anything in the methods of science itself, or in the spirit of science, which can help in the making of [political] decisions. . . . Is there anything we can learn from the relevance of science to politics? If we are to answer these questions, and answer them honestly, we must recognize important and basic differences between problems of science and problems of action, as they arise in personal or political life. If we fail to recognize these differences, we shall be seeking magic solutions and not real ones.[4]

This chapter looks at Oppenheimer's distinction between "realities" and values as far as this affected him as a scientist. That theme is tangled up with the subject of the next chapter—the *value* of curiosity—in which part of the point has to be that "realities," or truth, or science, have some intrinsic value, set apart from their extrinsic moral or political value. There is also a continuity with the previous chapter, in that we may get nearer to an understanding of the *kind* of decision that Oppenheimer made in 1942.

James Tuck, a British physicist who worked on the Manhattan Project, wrote that "Here at Los Alamos I found a spirit of Athens, of Plato, of an ideal Republic."[5]

Most of this chapter will be taken up with the modern discussion of facts and values—or science and politics. It should be useful to begin from one clear, if not immediately appealing, alternative: a model offered by Plato. His general intentions—so far as it can be meaningful to talk about them—were left open. His model state in the *Republic* might have been constructed as a purely ideal city, or as a serious practical proposal, or as an exemplar for political debate, or as an image of the human psyche, or even as some kind of satire (or some combination of all these). Whatever the intentions behind some of his weirder political prescriptions, there can be little doubt that they served as challenges to the contradictions and uncertainties that he must have disliked in contemporary thought and practice. Few people could ever have agreed with him. Perhaps he never wanted them to. But the reasons why they have disagreed have been important and productive.

Plato despised democratic decision-making. At the heart of his case in the *Republic*, instead of using direct argument he relied on a story about a crew on a ship arguing about navigation (VI, 488). His dismissive view was that the outcome could only be corruption, violence, and disaster. The ignorant crew would be certain to distrust a captain trained in scientific navigation. The whole story is oddly unsatisfying. (Why, for example, assume that sailors would be so self-destructively stupid?) But the upshot seems plain enough. Knowledge is needed to direct the ship of state: knowledge possessed by a few and suspected by the many. For Plato, those who would have the appropriate knowledge would be the philosopher-kings who had completed the curriculum outlined in Book VII of the *Republic*: not a training in political skills but an education in pure science. The practice of government required qualifications that would be limited to the ruling elite. Enlightenment was essential for a few but dangerous for the many. That limitation was significant because partial or incomplete education would be as disqualifying as none at all. Full understanding, crucially, could only be attained in the light of the idea of the good that was said to be the cause [*aitia*] (VI, 508e) of knowledge and truth.

Some themes emerge fairly plainly. Decisions in the state are to be taken by those who are relevantly qualified. Their qualifications will not merely include some attention to ethics, as if it were one of the subjects in a curriculum. The knowledge they possess will somehow derive from the good. This can be seen in two senses. In one, the search for knowledge acquires a motivation. Plato framed the desire for knowledge in the most passionate terms (VI, 490b). In another, knowledge cannot be ethically neutral.

Unfortunately, to have said this much is to have said very little. The nature of Plato's good has always seemed hopelessly elusive. His use of storytelling and imagery rather than argument seems to press against a limit of intelligibility, as he may have realized himself. In the *Republic*, the only discussion on the nature of the good peters out in irony (VI, 509c). A true interpretation of his central imagery might be available only to a god (VII, 517b). Plato's rulers were, effectively, scientists. But science uninformed by the good was harmfully incomplete. The rulers of the *Republic* would *see* what should be done because their science was moral as well as natural and because their educated vision would give them a direct view of truth or reality. They would be fully awake, not just dreaming (VII, 520).

The drawbacks in all this may be more evident than the advantages. A single good—or agreement on a single good—seems absurdly unlikely. The whole project of entrusting moral disagreements in society to the educated moral vision of a ruling class is so unappealing that it appears to need no debate. How far this may be taken as critical of Plato depends on how far the prescriptions in the *Republic* can have been intended practically, which must remain extremely uncertain.

In a Platonic state, but in wholly anachronistic terms, there would be no distinction between science and politics because politics would be a science and the rulers would be scientists. That seems least alarming as a possibility when "science" delivers results that are uncontroversially true or correct. No one should be offended when decisions on drainage in a city are taken by drainage experts. When this may not happen—where, for example, better drains are provided for the rich than for the poor—there may indeed be cause for complaint that politics has usurped the place of science. Here the sense of "politics" would be purely negative.

More controversially, in modern democratic societies, the appointment of an economically unqualified politician as minister of finance is not seen as too strange. The appointment of an economically unqualified chief of a central reserve bank might seem stranger. The assumption might be that some degree of economic knowledge is needed for that job. Presumably, in a Platonic state, the minister of finance would also have an ideal knowledge of economics and would make decisions in accord not with the democratic will but with the truth about the economy (the "realities").

Plato becomes still more uncomfortable for us with examples of truly specialized scientific expertise. Genetically modified crops must be either harmful or not harmful to us and to the environment, and there ought to be some correct method to decide one way or the other. It seems perverse that "political" decision-making on their use becomes unavoidable because of a shortage of knowledge or disagreements among partial experts. The role of politics becomes recognizable in a form that Plato particularly disliked: to act as a jury in choosing which witnesses to trust.

The underlying point is not obscure. To the extent that we can bring ourselves to regard an area as factual or scientific—and this needs no sophisticated definition now—we may be satisfied to see decisions made by qualified experts. Economics might be in that condition, though large parts of it are plainly not. (There is also the Keynesian view that important economics cannot be separated from political economy: itself a long way toward a Platonic integration of facts and means with ends and values.) Where economists are uncertain, or when they disagree, political arbitration may be needed. So "politics" seems to be a product of either ignorance or disagreement. One thought to be drawn from Plato is the oddity of that conclusion.

The Platonic state did have an army. The development and acquisition of weaponry would have to be a matter of military science, entrusted to those who knew about it. They would take their decisions in the light of their vision of the good for the state. The opinions of the citizenry would not be relevant. Nor—as with any of these examples—would there be any useful distinction between ends and means. The good of (or for) the state should be unambiguous: as much a matter of knowledge, not opinion, as any other question, and always to be answered in terms of the good of the whole, never the interests of the parts (VII, 519e).

From all of this, the Platonic challenge is: Why not? Must a distinction between fact and value coincide politically with a distinction between the settled and the contested? Must the political always be negative or residual: required only because of a lack of reliable knowledge, a deficit of trust, or some irremovable disagreement over ends or means? Plato's strongly positive account of politics forces us to ask how we can defend the distinctions he repudiated.

By 1945, atomic bombs were going to be completed. Development was not going to stop because of any individual's scruples. By that stage, no individual would have been essential to the completion of the project. The use of the first bombs was a matter for lengthy and complicated discussion. Oppenheimer played a large but not decisive part in that discussion. In 1945, a schism was apparent between the fact of the bombs and the choices to be made on their use. The respective roles of scientists (as "advisors") and politicians (as "decision-makers") seemed relatively clear, though this was far from universally agreed.

This book concentrates on 1942, when it had already been decided—by Roosevelt—to develop atomic weapons, though the extent of the eventual cost and the vast scale of the work were not foreseen.

The simple facts of the physics were widely known (though all the crucial details were not). Many physicists and a sizeable part of government machinery were already engaged in the initial steps. The question for Oppenheimer was whether he should take on responsibility for the necessary research. The factors that led to his decision, and to the decisions of many others, were never unclear. As many knew, the threat of an atomic bomb in Nazi hands seemed real enough. Later, the known work of Heisenberg seemed to make this more concrete. In 1942, if there was some schism between facts and values it would have been between the fact of the research (and possible development) that was going to take place and, for Oppenheimer, the rightness of taking a leading part in it.

That can be reduced to the clear and simplified terms of conventional philosophical debate, harking back to a blunt contrast between what *is* the case and what *ought* to be done. Coldly: atomic bombs, at any stage in their planning or development, were nothing but morally neutral physical objects, "neither moral nor immoral—they are just piles of chemicals, metals and junk."[6] Their value for good or evil lay entirely in their potential use by people and in their feelings toward them. (The same line of thinking is applied to guns, as in the mantra of the National Rifle Association: "Guns don't kill people; people kill people." The difference of scale in potential harm might not be seen as logically relevant.)

An opposed case might be argued in two steps. First, it could be denied that any weapon designed and defined to cause harm is morally neutral. So the alleged split between the physical facts and human feelings is misjudged. Second, it could be conceded that this is hard to argue in more modest cases—a penknife or a hunting rifle—but that it must apply to anything as certainly destructive as atomic weapons.

Nothing important hinges on whether atomic weapons are or are not said to be intrinsically good, bad, or neutral. No one could disagree that they are extremely dangerous to extremely large numbers of people and that this is undeniably part of their intrinsic character. That is what such weapons are for, after all. Oppenheimer said in November 1945 that "we have made a thing that by all the standards of the world we grew up in is an evil thing" and "There are people who say that they are not such very bad weapons. Before the New Mexico test we sometimes said that too, writing down square miles and equivalent tonnages and looking at the pictures of a ravaged Europe. After the test we did not say it any more."[7]

You can, if you like, *say* that a weapon capable of obliterating cities is value-free in itself, just as a natural phenomenon like small-pox or bubonic plague is value-free. It is hard to see what is gained or what sense is added by "intrinsic" or "in itself" in these terms, as though there was any point in thinking of weaponry—or the knowledge needed to create it—apart from its actual or potential use. (Although Oppenheimer himself went on to say that the atomic bomb is "a weapon for aggressors, and the elements of surprise and of terror are as intrinsic to it as are the fissionable nuclei.")

Such sterility shows up the comparative interest in Plato's apparently cranky account. Although the answers he gave were, to say the least, disturbing, the questions he suggested were surely sound. Not, for example, *whether* the possession of knowledge was connected with power and value, but *how*. Not *whether* knowledge was restricted in society, but *who* should possess and control it. This was not a sociology of knowledge as much as a political theory of knowledge. There is some irony in the fact that a famously unworldly theorist should present such sharp practical questions. In fact, the enlightenment dream of an open, free marketplace in knowledge was far more detached from any possible reality. Despite the wishes of many of the Los Alamos scientists, everything about the atomic bomb project was regarded as highly secret. The knowledge belonged to the U.S. government who had, after all, paid a great deal for it. The possession of that knowledge was regarded as an immense military and political asset. In no sense was it value-free.

Oppenheimer himself must have accepted the conventional modern division between advisors and decision-makers. (As quoted earlier, he did say, rather implausibly, "I was not in a policy-making position at Los Alamos."[8]) The usual justification lay in some idea of legitimacy for important decision-making. A democratic mandate conferred the right to decide. It was not conferred by knowledge, however expert. In 1942, the decision was, in any event, not one within any definition of pure science: to commit vast resources of personnel and money in pursuit of atomic weapons. The scale of the commitment was remarkable given the complete uncertainty of the outcome. The decision was political in the plain sense that it was made, without doubt, by one politician, Roosevelt, who had a constitutional right to make it.

But, in a different sense, how was there any distinction between that political decision and the decisions taken by Oppenheimer and his colleagues when choosing to take part in the project? They might well have contrasted their technical, scientific, factual work on the project itself with their initial decisions and continuing commitments. The one might be "scientific," the others in some sense "political" or "moral." All reports of Oppenheimer's actions at Los Alamos indicate that once he had launched himself into the work, with whatever thoughts in his mind, he never hesitated in carrying it through. Whether he underwent private reservations is, surely, irrelevant.[9] "Were such political and moral issues appropriate concerns for Manhattan Project scientists, who, after all, lacked training in these subjects?" asked one historian.[10] What is to be understood by *political* or *moral* in this context, and can that understanding be sustained? What "training" would be appropriate, who would get it, and who would decide who would get it?

The crucial question is, again, one in which Plato is suggestive. His good was the cause [*aitia*] of knowledge and truth. It "provides" [*parechei*] them, yet exceeds them in beauty (VI, 508e–509a). That is scarcely clear, except on the central matter of priority. The value of knowledge is not added or decided afterward. It must come first. There was a natural reflection in Plato's educational politics. Knowledge that did not derive from his good was worse than no knowledge at all.

In current terms, this can lead us to ask how far it is defensible to regard the political or the moral as consequent from the factual or scientific. The simplest model implies that here are the facts and then we have to decide what to do with them. (And a more sophisticated version, elaborated in terms of "supervenience," adds little extra.) Here is a neutral piece of atomic weaponry; then there is the "moral" question of what to do with it: Oppenheimer's "realities" against his "lights and values." Richard Feynman (who worked at Los Alamos) wrote bluntly that "ethical values lie outside the scientific realm." It is possible to ask how far that detached (and then subordinate) location for a moral choice is justifiable. Feynman based his insulation of ethical values on a distinction between means and ends. First you find out what will or can happen, then you decide what you "want" to happen. "Well, how do you know you don't want people killed? You see, at the end you must have some ultimate judgment." If, as Feynman argued lucidly, there is "an independence," then his conclusion may have been inevitable.[11]

Ernest Gellner suggested that the opening of a "chasm" between fact and value might have had roots in "any society endowed with science, i.e. sustained, cumulative, consensual exploration of nature by the experimental method, with the aid of mathematical formulations and rendered independent of social dogma and requirement. Under such conditions, and perhaps under such conditions only, the separation of fact and value becomes hard or impossible to avoid."[12] The difficulty in this kind of explanation is that it might work just as well in the opposite direction, where a separation of fact from value would be a necessary condition for scientific inquiry rather than a consequence. Maybe we should think of corollaries instead of causes in either direction.

The right way to disagree with Feynman is surely not to take a view that physical objects—bombs, for example—themselves possess or imply intrinsic values. It must be to question the order of priority whereby values, ends, or choices are left over as residual questions after the facts, science, or means have been settled. That ordering accepts that choice in morality or politics is essentially dependent on either ignorance or unresolvable disagreement. Where there are facts, they can be known. Otherwise, there may be choices. More fundamentally, the domain of the moral or political will be defined in residual terms, as what is left over from the factual or scientific. *Because* a correct answer to a question is not determinable, it becomes uncertain, hence debatable, hence a matter of choice. One implication is that the domain of the ethical or political is destined to shrink as knowledge grows. This is what scientifically inclined economists would like to think. The scope for political choice diminishes as economic expertise develops. Another implication is that correct ethical or political answers become impossible by definition. They will become only matters of opinion.

The most conspicuous modern dissenter from this picture was Emmanuel Levinas, who insisted darkly throughout his writings that *l'éthique* took—or should take—priority over what he called ontology. *Le Bien avant l'être.*[13] To appeal to his work may be to illuminate the obscure by the even more obscure; but his central insight seems to have been that I can only exist in a context of a relation to another person, a relation that he saw as intrinsically ethical—a matter of unavoidable "responsibility."

A parallel line of thinking is found in lower-key terms in Charles Taylor's *Sources of the Self,*[14] where I understand myself only through a shared language that embodies an inescapably moral framework. One route to that conclusion is through a linguistic argument, to the effect that a use of factual or representative language is not basic but, rather, is itself a special case of a wider use of language as expression. So factual description is not the basic use for language. This approach only impresses when you can be convinced that you can only understand one form of discourse (e.g., "scientific") if you understand another form (expressive-language-in-general). There seems no more reason to accept this constraint than the opposite view, the basis for positivist theories of meaning.

Levinas, writing in an altogether different idiom, was more elusive. It is clear where he stood on both the priority of the ethical and on its independence. It had to come first, and it could not be detachable. As an assertion—or as wishful thinking—this is plain enough. Its justification—against, for example, the kind of blunt approach just quoted from Feynman—was opaque. Levinas made a number of attempts, but the firmness of his conclusions was more striking than the force of the arguments that should have led to them. He maintained that "Western philosophy" had tried to neutralize and flatten "otherness," reducing "the Other" to "the Same." Any relation with "the Other" had to be intrinsically ethical, grounded in a basic relationship of responsibility, in which I stand as a "hostage" to another person. Much of the weight of argument was carried by a metaphor of *le visage*: the face. Otherness was epitomized in a face-to-face relationship that creates an "ethical" confrontation.

The full supporting case began from a view that the isolated self of the modern epistemological tradition was itself not ethically neutral. " 'I think' comes down to 'I can'—to an appropriation of that which is, to an exploitation of reality. Ontology as first philosophy is a philosophy of power."[15] The point asserted by Feynman, more starkly than by many philosophers, was that what happens can be regarded as independent of what you want to happen. Apparently, I can imagine myself in a value-free or ethically neutral world. Assuming a principle in which what you can imagine or represent may be regarded as possible (in some sense), it follows that values may be independent. Levinas denied not only this, but even that a representation of an isolated self could be available.

These are only the sketches of opposed positions so far apart that any contrast between them has to be contrived. That is because the intentions were so different. Feynman was thinking of outside interference in research. Science was taken as a distinct activity. "Politics" was external to it. There were excellent reasons for his view, brought to a head sharply in his dissenting report on the *Challenger* disaster of

1986: "For a successful technology, reality must take precedence over public relations, for nature cannot be fooled."[16] The starting-point of Levinas was entirely different. He had no interest in science. His concern was the experienced root of morality in a world where there was none. The implicit background was Jewish history in Europe from 1933 to 1945. His question was not a linguistic or logical one, about the grounding of ethical statements, but one that he might have seen as more primitive: the origin of morality when, in an entirely nontheoretical sense, no morality exists. *Totalité et Infini* opens melodramatically by asserting that the state of war suspends morality, asking: "Does not lucidity—the opening of the spirit on to the truth—consist in glimpsing the permanent possibility of war?" Later, he saw war as a condition where *les êtres* "reject community, reject the law; no frontier keeps one from the other nor defines them."[17] In hypothetical terms (which Levinas might not himself accept), the thought seems to have been that *if* there is to be morality, then its grounding has to be anterior to knowledge, not something left as a residue after factual matters have been settled.

Leaving aside the justification for that view, it seems natural to interject by inquiring: what indeed if there is no morality, since we can at least *imagine* a world without it? (That sounds analogous to a challenge imagined by Kant, presented by a person who is completely indifferent to morality. Kant could only respond with an unconvincing appeal to a sense of fear.[18]) But what *would* such a world be like? Not "neutral" but possibly—the thought from Levinas—a concentration camp. The fable of a value-free world of pure fact may well be a nightmare, not because it is impossible but because it could be all too possible. To imagine away morality is not to imagine a morally neutral world.

The order of thinking turns out to be what matters. To start with the ("scientific") facts and to regard value as what is left as unfactual means that facts are, by definition, value-free. The location of an opposed starting point is less clear. It could be, as for Levinas, an assumption that people stand in an irreducibly ethical relation to one another; or, more inarticulately, that the relations between people are what constitute ethics, if anything does. A view that might be defended more readily is that a distillation of pure facts is not only impossible but is itself value-loaded. Any statement of factual alternatives must presuppose judgments of relevance or significance that cannot themselves be purely factual: more on this shortly. Another productive line of argument comes from a hard look at the sterility of a logic of politics that might be based on a clear isolation of value from facts and ends from means. A literal conclusion would be that what we know is neutral, while what we care about is a matter of opinion. So experts advise, politicians decide. Political or moral decision would be reduced to choices made, literally, in ignorance. An unsurprising consequence might be an admiration for the prestige of expertise and a downgrading of politics.

There is an analogy with the previous chapter, which argued how misleading it could be to present a significant personal choice simply in terms of what to do next, with a past life taken for granted. The political version presents the known facts as given options and demands a verdict or decision.

The atomic bomb eroded this negative picture. By 1945, "moral debate" on the use of the bomb was shadow-boxing. The prospects that politicians could resist its use were nil, and so the scruples of powerless scientists were as irrelevant as the scientists felt them to be. In 1942 and 1943, when the bomb was still only an idea backed by a great deal of money, this may not have been so. Then, the question was not: Here *is* one large fact, what *should* be done with it now? But: *whether, how, who?* One of the reasons why Oppenheimer is important is that without him there might have been no bomb by August 1945. More certainly, and more to the point now, another is that when he chose to start the work on the bomb in 1942, he seemed to cross a boundary between physical theory and political engagement. He is significant, not merely as a general symbol but as an actual individual, because he was the first to take this step so dramatically. Others had been working on the feasibility of the bomb since 1940, but it was Oppenheimer who took on the leadership of the project when the choice to turn it into a reality had been made. He is sometimes berated for a seemingly frivolous dismissal of the seriousness of that step, for example, by Jonathan Glover, quoting (twice, in two separate books) from an interview of Oppenheimer with Robert Jungk:

> It is my judgment in these things that when you see something that is technically sweet you go ahead and do it and you argue what to do about it only after you have had your technical success. That is the way it was with the atomic bomb. I do not think anyone opposed making it; there were some debates about what to do with it after it was made.[19]

This was a retrospective remark in a hostile context. There was never any doubt what the atomic bomb was for, as Oppenheimer and all his colleagues knew as well as anyone in 1942: to cause huge damage and death. What damage and whose death were not known, but the point of the weapon was no secret. Oppenheimer's remark sounds like a macabre caricature of an opposition between fact and value. There was the "technical sweetness" and then there were the "debates about what to do with it." Such provocativeness may have sounded persuasive afterward, but things can never have been so straightforward. Self-evidently, in 1945, without the fact of a bomb there would have been no question of choices about whether it could be used. There was never a value-free choice, even before 1942. The purely "technical" question would have to be something like: will this work? (And how far pure curiosity is valid as a motive is the subject of the next chapter.) In 1942, there had to be some other question to provide a degree of motivation, such as: are we going to find out if this works? That question was answered first by the theorists at Los Alamos and then in practice at Alamogordo. It was asked at first not by physicists but by the politicians who financed and supported them. The bomb is implausible as pure fact not simply because it was a project in applied, not pure, science. Shall (not even *should*) we do this? can never be a question of pure fact; but, without asking it, there can be no pursuit of facts, pure or otherwise.

Once again, as in the previous chapter, the reduction, or simplification, of a problem to yes or no repudiates the prior question of how that point was reached or how the alternatives came to be crystallized. And again, to say this is not to shuffle responsibility from the choosing agent to a vaguer history. Oppenheimer knew, far better that his critics, that the "technical" question of the bomb in 1942—would it work?—may have come before the question of how the bomb was to be used, but it came after the question of whether the bomb was going to be made. He knew, again, far better than his critics, that his influence on the use of the bomb was limited by 1945, but also what had led to the decisions to proceed with "technical" development before 1942. In personal terms, a choice of actions could never have been seen fairly as value-free—a purely technical pursuit of instrumental means. In the political context, the choice of ends could never have been described in 1942 as independent of practical realities. At no level is a schism between the facts and values of the case plausible.

Where does this get us in practical terms? Surely, in Feynman's impatient meaning, the position of Oppenheimer in 1942 was clear enough. Whether he wanted, or felt obliged, to take on the leadership of bomb research was a simple issue. He could have refused. The factors that led him to accept—whether personal ambition, a flagging career, patriotism, or curiosity—were recognizably not technical factors, such as whether the bomb would work, or could be made in time at a feasible cost.

The compartmentalization that insists on a separation between the "technical sweetness" of a scientific problem and the rightness of a political choice has to be understood, not simply frowned on. It allows for a denial of autonomy: at the extreme "only obeying orders"; less radically, a blurring of responsibility. An easy point to forget is that Plato's politicized view of knowledge in the *Republic* took this into account. The question of who should be in charge was the same as the question of who should possess knowledge. The expert without an insight into the good should not be allowed political power. This was banal if read in our terms, as a recommendation that scientists should be put in charge of the state, or that politicians should be made to take courses in ethics. A more negative or critical understanding can make sense: Practical questions of who should possess knowledge cannot be separated from questions of power; questions of knowledge cannot be separated from questions of value. The immediate complaint will either be to deny that this must be so or to ask why it should be accepted. One answer can be to point to the price of denying or ignoring it. The point sounds uninformatively tautologous: separate values from facts and you end up with an alienation of political or moral choices from technical realities. Maybe so, but this can still be informative.

In the *Republic*, all opinions were personalized. No theories were discussed in the abstract; only the views of the named participants in an after-dinner meeting. The political questions can be seen as personal. There is power in the state: Who is to hold it? Knowledge will exist and will confer advantage and power: Who is to have it? Plato raised and answered both questions together, by making legitimacy and (what we call) educational qualification personally interdependent—personally meaning in the same hands. He did not just think, conventionally, that rulers should be well advised—that committees of the best scientists should be assembled—but that rulers themselves should literally know what they were doing. (His own dismal experience as a political consultant in Syracuse may have been relevant.) The drawback—as amply underlined in the *Republic*—was more than a little absurdity. Philosopher-kings were and are, after all, deeply implausible, then as now, as Plato knew well. The other side was seen from the problem in the alternative: dissociation between ends and means or values and facts. Trained politicians may seem unpalatable for various reasons, but are they less unpalatable than untrained politicians? The choice may not be as unlikely as it sounds, given the reality of dealing with scientific development. The Manhattan Project may have been scientifically and technically formidable, but it was less impressive as an alliance of political will with practical ingenuity. The alienation between those who understood the project and those who made decisions was almost complete. Truman, who made the final decisions on the use of the bomb, did not even know of its existence only four months before: not Platonic satire, but political reality.

CHAPTER FOUR

CURIOSITY

In the years after 1945, Oppenheimer spoke a good deal on the value of knowledge and the force of scientific curiosity. For example, in his farewell speech at Los Alamos: "when you come right down to it the reason that we did this job is because it was an organic necessity. If you are a scientist you cannot stop such a thing. If you are a scientist you believe that it is good to find out how the world works" and from a symposium on Atomic Energy later in 1945: "Because we are scientists . . . it is our faith and our commitment, seldom made explicit, even more seldom challenged, that knowledge is a good in itself, knowledge and such power as may come with it."[1] Science has an intrinsic value. Research is propelled figuratively by its own momentum—"you cannot stop such a thing."

In the sharpest contrast, Groves wrote in his memoirs:

> My rule was simple and not capable of misinterpretation— each man should know everything he needed to know to do his job and nothing else . . . it made quite clear to all concerned that the project existed to produce a specific end product—not to enable individuals to satisfy their curiosity and to increase their scientific knowledge.[2]

He was thinking of his security headaches at Los Alamos, but the directness of what he said is striking. The research was not at all a matter of "curiosity" as far as he was concerned. Nor was its value intrinsic. It was related to a "specific end product." It had a value, too. It was, literally, very expensive.

Oppenheimer's line can be seen as implicitly apologetic. It is the value of knowledge that drives science. Whether this made an effective defense of research into atomic weapons—and Groves's remark sounds a harsher counterpoint—it remains of great importance in scientific ideology. Knowledge must, and will, be pursued. (Edward Teller, bluntly, in 1947: "The development of pure and applied science cannot and must not be stopped."[3]) There may be other motives behind research—desires to defeat enemies, trump competitors, win prizes, improve careers—all entirely understandable, but the purest motive is, or should be, curiosity about "how the world works." To the scientist, this conviction may matter. The *motives* behind research may be personal, noble, ignoble, mercenary, or high-minded, but a *good reason* for research will always be the pursuit of knowledge.

Groves's sharpness gives one answer to questions about the intrinsic value of science. The point of research at Los Alamos was military. That is why it was funded. If the motives of individuals that kept them working were not military, then that did not matter as long as the result was the same. Nevertheless, Oppenheimer's view can still be seen as the basic justification for individual participation in the work. And there is a very clear paradox. The previous chapter looked at the separation of the "realities" of research from the "lights and values" of politics (and those words come from the same speech in November 1945). The facts of science were value-neutral. Values were for others: for politicians. But now we see the opposite. Knowledge has some kind of higher value, which means that it must be pursued. This value was crucial in the pursuit of science. More rhapsodically, from 1953: "A great discovery is a thing of beauty; and our faith—our binding, quiet faith—is that knowledge is good and good in itself."[4] Or from 1945 again: "It is not possible to be a scientist unless you believe that the knowledge of the world, and the power which this gives, is, a thing which is of intrinsic value to humanity."[5] What sort of value was this, and how defensible was it? What would be the alternatives?

◆

"There were many scientists for whom the German factor was the main motivation," wrote Joseph Rotblat, who left Los Alamos in 1944. "Why did they not quit when this factor ceased to be? The most frequent reason given," he claimed, "was pure and simple scientific

curiosity—the strong urge to find out whether the theoretical calculations and predictions would come true. These scientists felt that
only after the test at Alamogordo should they enter into the debate
about the use of the bomb."[6]

Curiosity—the desire for knowledge—may be seen as natural,
almost biological: a strong urge, as Rotblat called it. Small children,
even animals, seem naturally full of curiosity. It is remarkably hard to
be uncurious if you have a curious disposition. It may seem natural to
keep asking questions like "How does this work?" No justification may
seem necessary, any more than tastes—for football, opera, or Mexican
cuisine—need to be justified. But this will not do. If scientific curiosity
were no more than a personal taste for knowledge, it could scarcely be
cited with such confidence as reasoned support for inquiry. A difference
between a personal ambition and a pursuit of truth as an impetus for
research is not merely that the one sounds more respectable than the
other. It is that one is only a motive while the other offers—at least
ostensibly—a reason. To some extent, such a reason is not just personal, like a taste or an interest, but is, in some way, available to
anyone. "If you are a scientist, you believe that it is good to find out
how the world works" cannot just mean that it feels agreeable to you
to find out how the world works. It means that curiosity should be in
the character of any scientist.

The trouble is that scientific curiosity is very far from being a
universal trait, at any one time or across history, as in Aristotle's
bland assertion in the opening words of his *Metaphysics* that "all men
by nature desire to know." Whatever the justification for curiosity, it
certainly cannot be that human beings have some natural urge for a
certain type of explanatory knowledge. Even if that were so, it could
be asked *why* such an urge should be satisfied. Today there still survive
many societies in which the curiosity of visiting anthropologists is not
even puzzling to local inhabitants, but is simply of no interest. And
in the past, there were times when scientific inquiry was not viewed
as it is now. The period when it did rise to its later prestige is easy
enough to identify.

The *Confessions* of St Augustine contain a fierce denunciation of
unbridled curiosity:

> Beside the lust of the flesh which inheres in the delight given
> by all pleasures of the senses . . . there exists in the soul, through
> the medium of the same bodily senses, a cupidity which does

not take delight in carnal pleasure but in perceptions acquired through the flesh. It is a vain inquisitiveness dignified with the title of knowledge and science. As this is rooted in the appetite for knowing, and as among the senses the eyes play a leading role in acquiring knowledge, the divine word calls it "the lust of the eyes" (1 John 2: 16).

Earlier, and more mildly:

Lord God of truth, surely the person with a scientific knowledge of nature is not pleasing to you on that ground alone. The person who knows all those matters but is ignorant of you is unhappy. The person who knows you, even if ignorant of natural science, is happy. Indeed the one who knows both you and nature is not on that account happier. You alone are his source of happiness if knowing you he glorifies you for what you are and gives thanks and is not lost in his own imagined ideas (Romans 1: 21).[7]

The value of inquisitiveness—curiosity—was seen at best as in need of being tempered, or kept in proportion with other values. (Referring to Augustine, Heidegger tried to distinguish curiosity from wonder; but this meant too plainly just that he disapproved of one but not the other.[8]) It may seem easy to decry Augustine's approach as a wish to stifle or censor research, but he certainly should not be dismissed as crudely antiscientific. It is reasonable enough to ask why one value— curiosity or, more positively, free research—should take priority over others. An appeal to what seems natural is obviously inadequate. (And an appeal to pragmatic effectiveness could not be more ironically circular than with the Manhattan Project: curiosity was valuable because it brought the atomic bomb.) There is no need to accept Augustine's position: only to see that it is a tenable one. Within what cannot be denied as "Western thought," a primacy for scientific inquisitiveness was not inevitable.

Equally, there can be little doubt that the intellectual framework that supported curiosity as a value was constructed and ramified over a short period in Europe in the seventeenth century. The work of Galileo and Bacon hardened into an ideology for Descartes and his contemporaries and was systematized into a dogma by Spinoza. In the work of Malebranche, "natural" curiosity was vindicated as a search for divine truth. A section in his *Search after Truth* entitled "Curiosity is natural and essential" began:

> So long as men have an inclination for a good that surpasses their strength and that they do not possess, they will always have a secret inclination for anything that seems novel and extraordinary. They will constantly pursue things to which they have given no consideration, in the hope of finding what they search for in them; and since their mind can never be entirely satisfied except through the perception of Him for whom they were made, they will always be in a state of restlessness and agitation until He appears to them in His glory.[9]

Later, the General Scholium of Newton's *Principia* became the most well-known scientific creed. As early as 1647, the French Preface to Descartes's *Principles of Philosophy* set out an incredibly confident manifesto, considering that the enterprise of successful discovery had only been under way for a few decades. A claim was staked out for the superiority to be derived from science (here called philosophy). Despite the lofty Platonic tone, there was also a more mundane hint that science pays:

> we should consider that it is this philosophy alone which distinguishes us from the most savage and barbarous peoples, and that a nation's civilization and refinement depends on the superiority of the philosophy which is practiced there. Hence the greatest good that a state can enjoy is to possess true philosophers.

There are passages in the Preface that can only be seen as salesmanship of the most bombastic, flattering kind:

> No soul, however base, is so strongly attached to the objects of the senses that it does not sometimes turn aside and desire some other, greater good, even though it may often not know what this good consists in. Those who are most favored by fortune and possess health, honor and riches in abundance are no more exempt from this desire than anyone else. On the contrary, I am convinced that it is just such people who long most ardently for another good—a good higher than all those

they already possess. Now this supreme good, considered by natural reason without the light of faith, is nothing other than the knowledge of the truth through its first causes, that is to say wisdom, of which philosophy is the study. Since these points are absolutely true, they would easily carry conviction if they were properly argued.

Indeed, they might carry conviction, but they were not properly argued here. The assertion that even the rich naturally crave for scientific knowledge was so brazen that it can only be seen as an attempt to establish a point by suggestive wishful thinking. The philosophy that everyone wants will be successful. Descartes promised that its principles will "enable us to deduce the knowledge of all the other things to be found in the world," admittedly not quite yet, but eventually.[10] Its success would be built on the use of his method and would rely on the interconnectedness of knowledge. Basic facts would lead to less basic facts until we have all facts.

Because so much of Descartes's manifesto turned out to be so productive, there is a temptation to pass over its frail foundations. He produced nothing to support his sales pitch for the "supreme good." If this meant anything, it must have been that his preferred type of knowledge was not just good—scarcely worth arguing—but better than anything else. The fact that he may have been relying on suppressed Platonic premises—a hierarchy of goods, an identity between truth and goodness—did nothing to save the shakiness of the position. The kind of value or supreme good that he had in mind was left unexplained. Those "favored by fortune" might be impressed by the potential enhancement of their "nation's civilization and refinement," but that sort of payoff might not impress everyone. Extraordinary quantities of connected facts were discovered in the subsequent centuries by the pursuit of methodical inquiry (if not altogether along Cartesian lines). These facts were extraordinarily profitable. An economic chasm did open between their discoverers and those "savage and barbarous peoples" who were less well informed.

Descartes was plainly right that science would pay off, but there were two important weak points of principle in his approach. Despite his assertive tone, he had no justification for his "supreme good." Taken, as it must be, as a statement of value, it sounds unlikely. To his contemporary audience, it should have been heresy. Scientific curiosity (or any other form) had never been blessed in the canon of christian virtues. Its high ranking as a "good" received support only within a Platonic framework that Descartes treated with reservation elsewhere. Nietzsche noted sharply:

> In antiquity the dignity and recognition of science were diminished by the fact that even her most zealous disciples placed the striving for *virtue* first, and one felt that knowledge had received the highest praise when one celebrated it as the best means to virtue. It is something new in history that knowledge wants to be more than a mere means.[11]

Second, there was Descartes's characteristic reservation of natural reason "without the light of faith." The search for truth through science could not be comprehensive or unqualified. (It had theological constraints, filled out later in the circumspect treatment by Malebranche: his passage, quoted earlier and headed "Curiosity is natural and essential," was followed immediately by another headed "Three rules for controlling curiosity."[12]) For Descartes, there was the natural light of reason and there was the spiritual light of faith. The boundary between them was not to be discussed by him. (His main concern with theology was to keep well away from it, for reasons of prudence and perhaps genuine lack of interest.) But this could not do for long.

A more finished ideology was produced thirty years later by Spinoza. In an early work, the *Treatise on the Emendation of the Intellect*, after a routine repudiation of delusive goals such as fame and money, he announced that something permanent would be more satisfying. For him, the "supreme good" was to arrive at a "knowledge of the union which the mind has with the whole of Nature." A footnote promised further details, which never arrived because the work was left unfinished.[13] His definitive thinking appeared in the posthumous *Ethics*. There were two important steps beyond Descartes. First, teleology was abandoned completely. There were to be no ends or purposes in nature. Human ends or purposes were to be reinterpreted as desires. Desires, in turn, were grounded in a kind of basic drive or striving—Spinoza's *conatus*. A positive, salutary striving for human beings would be to increase their knowledge. A drive for knowledge was not a result of the attractive power of truth (in Platonic terms), but was a kind of urge that it is beneficial to cultivate. It would reduce passivity to external forces and increase activity or independence. Curiosity was a virtue not because it aims at a supreme good—there are no aims—but because it is, basically, good for you. You will be in a better state with more knowledge than with less, or none. And the sense of "better" was indeed deliberately ambiguous, between health and virtue.

There was also to be no limit to curiosity. Spinoza made no distinction between natural and supernatural knowledge. The object of all inquiry was *divina natura*, which can be taken as either divine nature or the divine nature, in line with his identification of God with nature—*Deus, sive natura.* "The highest virtue of the mind is to understand or to know God" or, of course, nature, without distinction. So: "for the man who is guided by reason, the final goal, that is, the highest desire whereby he strives to control all the others, is that by which he is brought to an adequate conception of himself and of all things that can fall within the scope of his understanding."[14] The important element in Spinoza's approach was the backing given to the unrestricted search for "causes" as a route to a full understanding of nature. There were to be no purposes in nature, no providence to be discerned or respected, and no meanings to delay the search for truth. Science could be pursued in a uniform and comprehensive way:

> Our approach to the understanding of the nature of things of every kind should be . . . one and the same; namely, through the universal laws and rules of nature . . . I shall, then, treat of the nature and strength of the emotions, and the mind's power over them, by the same method as I have used in treating of God and the mind, and I shall consider human actions and emotions just as if it were an investigation into lines, planes, or bodies.[15]

Why things were as they were was to be transparent. Descartes had treated the human body as a machine, to stress its intelligibility. The "rational soul" would need different treatment because it had been "specially created."[16] For Spinoza, God and the mind were to be as intelligible as the body. There were to be no barriers to understanding. Truth was to be available if sought.

Spinoza repudiated any distinction between causes and reasons, and so could not separate personal motives from allegedly impersonal justifications or excuses. The cause of curiosity is a drive for more knowledge; the reason for it may seem otherwise, but that may just be self-deception. Taken as an anthropological generalization—everyone feels scientific curiosity—his view about a natural striving towards more knowledge was simply false. The psychology was purely a priori. What he could have meant was that curiosity—a desire to increase knowledge—is beneficial for those who cultivate it. They will expe-rience a liberation from ignorance and its ill effects.

Spinoza's account may have been psychologically shrewd, or merely cynical. Reasons to act (in general) for him were fundamen-tally self-serving. His casual identification of a "final goal" with a "highest desire" can only be disconcerting. Yet there cannot be many alternative theories to explain or vindicate curiosity. Spinoza concen-trated on the curiosity of the researcher as a drive. Aristotle leant on natural inclination. The other main rival view might seem to be Platonic: to rest on the attractive power of the truth, or of knowledge. That would sound less self-centered, more disinterested. Actually, Plato's own thinking was not quite like that:

> it is the nature of the real lover of learning to struggle toward what is, not to remain with any of the many things which are believed to be . . . as he moves on he neither loses nor lessens his erotic love until he grasps the being of each nature itself with the part of his soul that is fitted to grasp it, because of its kinship with it, and that, once getting near what really is and having intercourse with it and having begotten under-standing and truth, he knows, truly lives, is nourished . . . [17]

The parallel in Plato to Spinoza's drive or *conatus* was the force of eros. It must be doubtful whether this could be modernized or demythologized without distortion. It may have been a signal that explanation had come to an end; a step from *logos* to *muthos*.

Groves wrote (as quoted at the beginning of this chapter) that the Manhattan Project "existed to produce a specific end product—not to enable individuals to satisfy their curiosity and to increase their scientific knowledge." He knew that curiosity may have been a drive behind the intellectual work of Oppenheimer's researchers. Clearly, his job was to keep this in the right channel. He knew that curiosity might be acceptable as a motive for scientific work, but it could hardly be taken politically as a reason or justification.

It would be wrong to impute any explicit theory of curiosity to Oppenheimer. He produced a good many ruminations on the future of science in the years after 1945, but he added nothing usefully new on its motivation. What he thought must be what he said laconically in 1945. It is fundamental that "it is good to find out how the world works." And "you cannot stop such a thing."

The latter view need not detain us long now. Responsibility is the subject of the next chapter and the irreversibility of scientific change will be the subject of chapter 6. There will be more discussion around the thought that you cannot stop. The view that, *literally*, research cannot be stopped does not need much discussion. It can be taken in several pragmatic senses: it is not practically possible to prevent research; if you do not do it, then someone else will; it should not be possible to restrain research; scientists themselves have difficulty in constraining their own activities. And so on, all justifiable to some degree. There is also the stronger view that science has some momentum of its own that drives it forward. If this means that scientists are not responsible for science because it has the autonomy of a Frankenstein's monster, then a great deal more justification is needed. Whatever the power of curiosity, it must be a long way short of being literally unavoidable or unstoppable.

It is harder to get a grasp on Oppenheimer's other remark: "If you are a scientist, you believe that it is good to find out how the world works." It is worth keeping in mind how important this is. Why science, for a scientist? Hume noted coolly: "tho' the exercise of genius be the principal source of that satisfaction we receive from the sciences, yet I doubt, if it be alone sufficient to give us any considerable enjoyment."[18] At least since the publication of *The Double Helix* by James Watson, there have been few illusions about the immaculate purity of the search for truth. Proper ambition, pride, vanity, competitiveness, envy, and a spectrum of other motivations all play a part. At Los Alamos there were also incitements from apprehension of a German bomb, desire to end the war, patriotism, concern for American science, loyalty to the project and to colleagues, and so on. Why, though, the sense that finding out how the world works was the justification "when you come right down to it"? Partly that this was the motivation specific to researchers, which distinguished them from all the others in the project. After all, Groves and his political masters were just as desperate as the scientists that the bomb at Alamogordo would work, and for many similar reasons. But for the researcher as well as personal motives or political loyalties there was disinterested investigation. Motivation did not have to be "pure" in a sense that it contained no personal factors, but the impersonal disinterest was what characterized research. The point of distinction was also the fine point of justification. This may well be reading too much into Oppenheimer's words; though it is striking that in his farewell speech at Los Alamos he did not cite either patriotism or victory in the war as "the reason that we did this job."

What sort of excuse, reason, or justification was this? Minimally, if the baseline of defense lay in the disinterest, it was a claim to unselfish, objective curiosity. How could that be supported? The most forthright thinker in this territory was Nietzsche. He addressed the "unconditional will to truth" in both *On the Genealogy of Morals* and Book V of *The Gay Science*—

> Science itself now *needs* a justification (which is not at all to say that there is one for it). On this question, turn to the most ancient and most modern philosophies: all of them lack a consciousness of the extent to which the will to truth itself needs a justification, here is a gap in every philosophy—how does it come about?[19]

—a fuller statement of the blunt question on the first page of *Beyond Good and Evil*: why not rather untruth? On two points he was very clear. Any "faith in science" could not be based in a "calculus of utility"—"It must have originated *in spite of* the fact that the disutility and dangerousness of "the will to truth," of "truth at any price" is proved to it constantly." Knowledge must be "more than a means"[20]—and there was nothing to be gained by appeals to "scientific" foundations—

> Strictly speaking, there is no "presuppositionless" knowledge, the thought of such a thing is unthinkable, paralogical: a philosophy, a "faith" always has to be there first, for knowledge to win from it a direction, a meaning, a limit, a method, a *right* to exist. (Whoever understands it the other way round and, for example, tries to place philosophy "on a strictly scientific foundation," needs first to *stand not only philosophy on its head* but truth itself as well . . .)[21]

The will to truth—more prosaically, curiosity or more forcefully, "the passion to know"[22]—is itself a value behind or within scientific inquiry, not something that follows from it. "Science itself never creates values."[23] Nietzsche maintained that that "moral ground" lay beneath the basic scientific attitude: "I will not deceive, not even myself." Whether this was a good or bad thing as far as he was concerned is not entirely clear. On the one side—"those who are truthful in that audacious and ultimate sense that is presupposed by the faith in science *thus affirm another world* than the world of life, nature, and history"—which would have to be taken as extremely critical, given his usual devotion to the "world of life." The suggestion was that faith in science must be extrascientific, with its origins in a history that might be expected to have attracted Nietzsche's scorn:

> it is still a *metaphysical faith* upon which our faith in science rests . . . even we seekers after knowledge today, we godless metaphysicians still take our fire, too, from the flame lit by a faith that is thousands of years old, that Christian faith which was also the faith of Plato, that God is the truth, that truth is divine.

Yet his approach was not uniformly negative. To realize how far a drive toward truth was itself imbued with value was itself to revalue it in a new light.[24]

There is no need to go all the way with Nietzsche to note the paradox in Oppenheimer's position. As seen in the previous chapter, the pursuit of science—"what the realities are"—was to be value-free. Yet science itself was dominated by a value: the value of knowledge as "a good in itself." This value explained and justified the activity. Nietzsche would see that as a matter of what he called "morality"— that is, as a set of beliefs whose origins can be sought and questioned. How can there be a convincing appeal to one overriding value—the value of truth—when other values are left for others to settle? There is a real contradiction, which should force the questions: What *is* the place of the value of truth among other values? And what explains it?

One answer is indeed that the apparent purity and compulsion of the motivation gain their force from a morality. The drive toward truth derives its plausibility in a resemblance to moral motivation on the Kantian model: overriding justification, disinterestedness, commitment. Nietzsche relied on "the ascetic ideal," but here that may be an unnecessary diversion. The accuracy of his "genealogy" of morality in this instance—"the faith of Plato" and so on—does not matter as much as the recognition that a value may stand in need of *some* basis, historical or otherwise.[25] Equally, if not more important is the issue of why some truths are supposed to matter more than others. The trouble with broad theoretical, psychological, or historical vindications of the value of truth, or our need for it, is that not all truths matter. In fact, most do not matter at all, at least in terms of interest or curiosity.

It is possible to push all this aside with a suspicion that any talk of knowledge as a good in itself was only a rhetorical mask for cruder considerations of military utility. Yet it may have been entirely correct that Oppenheimer and his colleagues at Los Alamos were not motivated in the end by questions of utility. Nietzsche was not denying that an elevated language of the love of truth may be in the minds of scientists, or that such language may be needed for motivation and justification. The problem was in its foundation. And again, the point was not that there can be none, but that it may not have been able to bear the load put on it. Nietzsche's "God is the truth" may only have been a concise version of the fulsome statement of Descartes, from earlier in this chapter: "this supreme good ... nothing other than the knowledge of the truth through its first causes, that is to say wisdom, of which philosophy is the study." Its advantage was that it disguised less. Descartes had nothing but hopeful rhetoric to hold up his "supreme good."

But so what? Back to Augustine, or Malebranche, when science is no doubt to be subordinated to some religious criteria or priorities. Nietzsche may seem an unlikely writer to call in aid of a sense of proportion, but that may be his most useful contribution here. We need to see first that curiosity does imply a value—maybe at the extreme, Oppenheimer's avowal of a value where "knowledge is a good in itself." Then we need to ask what kind of value this is. And then we need to ask what its place should be. Nietzsche was on firm ground, both in implying that none of this should be taken for granted and in denying that utilitarianism could provide satisfactory answers. In a predominantly optimistic age, his ferocious distrust of the benefits of nineteenth-century civilization was shared by very few. After 1945, it has seemed less certain that the gains from the unqualified—or rather narrowly directed—pursuit of truth will outweigh the losses, in large part because of what happened at Alamogordo, Hiroshima, and Nagasaki. The difficulty can be put back by one step by arguing that no one can estimate the value of an item of knowledge until it is discovered. So caution about the search for truth can do as much harm as good. So research must always, in principle, be open-ended. That would be to suggest that more knowledge may lead to more beneficial results rather than that knowledge is a good in itself. This may or may not be right, but the point at issue is one of the motivation or drive behind the search. No one could doubt that the science that succeeded Descartes's confident manifesto of 1647 was productive and largely useful. But even Descartes did not appeal directly to productivity and usefulness as the motivation for scientists. They were supposed to be "people who long most ardently for another good—a good higher than all those they already possess . . . this supreme good."

To be reduced to asking "but what are the alternatives?" is already to concede much of Nietzsche's case—that the value of a search for knowledge as a good in itself is not persuasive. If it were self-evident, why the need for the idealistic words about the supreme good?

Once again, the interest now is not in the benefits or the value of science, but in the force of the motivation. The history of a view that it must be overridingly compelling can be traced in outline. The history is thin and disappointing: in essence, little more than some ideological bluster from Descartes about the good of knowledge. But to appreciate that history does nothing to alter current feelings. I may wonder why I feel a drive toward scientific inquiry, discover that I have been brought up in a climate of Cartesian research, see the frailty of its foundations, yet still be as inquisitive as ever. If I think that a drive toward scientific inquiry needs moderation, an understanding of its origins may do nothing to achieve this. Stephen Toulmin has argued in his *Cosmopolis* that the mentality of the modern age would be (or would have been) healthier if it had found its origins in Montaigne rather than Descartes. There would be (or would have been) a wider, more humane, less mechanical perspective. Science would be placed in a less exposed context.[26] Even if that diagnosis were correct, it is hard to see what might follow in practice. Montaigne's own views on this subject sound notably unhelpful: "In Man curiosity is an innate evil, dating from his origins: Christians know that particularly well. The original Fall occurred when Man was anxious to increase his wisdom and knowledge: that path led headlong to eternal damnation. Pride undoes man; it corrupts him."[27] Someone eager for a career in science might become less inclined towards a hierarchical, reductive view, in which physics comes out as all-embracing top discipline. Someone assessing a research proposal might try to apply wider criteria. Scientists might be inflicted with more nonscientific education. The difficulties in such remedies must be obvious. Scientific curiosity must be a cultural rather than a biological phenomenon, but that does nothing to diminish its force. The creation, entrenchment, and revaluation of values cannot be simple or painless, as Nietzsche often emphasized.[28] A calm reappraisal of the intellectual status of the sciences was not what he had in mind.

Any discussion of curiosity—of the value of truth or knowledge and its disinterested pursuit—must touch on the issues raised in the previous chapter. By the time Malebranche was writing in terms of "controlling curiosity" in the middle of the seventeenth century the direction of debate was evident. Curiosity—the pursuit of truth—was natural, subject to necessary (theological) constraint. The model for knowledge was to be one of negative freedom—freedom was to be unlimited except where restraint could be argued. The assumption might have been that knowledge itself is value-free. Human choices determine which knowledge is to be pursued, and with what degree of enthusiasm.

On this reading, the apprehension that soon struck American and British physicists after Hahn's reports of his experiments in 1938–1939 was caused not by the facts of fission, or the potential facts of its further development, but by an understanding of decisions that might be taken about those facts, or lines of inquiry that might be pursued. It is reasonable to comment that this would show a partial view of what might count as neutrally factual. The facts of physics, for example, could be contrasted with the human choice to pursue them. But such pursuit only becomes unavoidable when the fact of untrammeled human curiosity is assumed to be unavoidable as well. No choice seems applicable here. This looks paradoxical, or inconsistent.

CHAPTER FIVE

RESPONSIBILITY

Oppenheimer chose to lead the research on the first atomic bombs, which were then used to kill a great many people in Hiroshima and Nagasaki. What can be said about his responsibility?

Naturally, there are historical questions that have received a good deal of attention. How large was Oppenheimer's contribution to the building of the first bombs? Would they have been built without him? How large was his contribution to debates and decisions on their use? These questions can be answered briefly, but not decisively. Oppenheimer's leadership of the Manhattan Project may have meant that it was completed in time for the first use of bombs in August 1945, though no one can know what would have happened if the work had taken much longer. The entry of the Soviet Union into the war with Japan at what turned out to be the last minute might have ended hostilities in any event, but this can be only speculative. Oppenheimer was a member of a committee that made specific recommendations on the use of the first bombs in Japan, and that reached the view that "the most desirable target would be a vital war plant employing a large number of workers and closely surrounded by workers' homes."[1] Roosevelt undoubtedly started the project and Truman undoubtedly made the final decision on its use, and was more straightforward than anyone about his responsibility.

Responsibility for the development and use of the first atomic bombs was diffuse. Einstein discovered the necessary theory. Hahn, Szilard, Lawrence, Oppenheimer, and many others made the necessary links between theory and implementation. Groves, Bush, Conant, and the rest of the administrative-political hierarchy concentrated the necessary resources. Toward the end of the project, the military moved in on debates about how the bomb was to be used.

To the historian, the question of who played a part, and to what extent, is central: who attended meetings, made recommendations, took decisions. This chapter looks at connected, but wider questions, about the place of the individual in the first steps in a large project. More than the previous chapters, it is a study in the conventional, abstract themes of moral philosophy: responsibility, judgment, intention, agency, the significance of consequences. But these are also themes that must bear on one individual, to the extent that there seems little value in thinking about them if they do not. There can be no point in an abstract account of moral themes unless it can be related convincingly to a real case. This should also reflect on us, now. A central question must be: How, if at all, is judgment possible? That is: What is it for us now to think about the responsibility for what happened in the past? Who are we to judge? Must there be judgment? What is its function? Here, the aim is certainly not to pass a verdict on Oppenheimer or to measure degrees of responsibility, still less guilt. Rather, it is to consider the place and meaning of such judgments or verdicts.

A fundamental issue is what happens to responsibility outside a simple textbook example of one person alone producing one action with one clear set of consequences. Philosophers' discussions of action and agency have tended to focus on issues of free and autonomous choice by one agent: What is the causality of an action? What prevents or excuses an agent from being assigned responsibility for an action? Where is the distinction between responsibility and guilt?[2] In Oppenheimer's case the difficult question is one of the meaning of responsibility in a situation in which causality or agency was so evidently shared. In this respect, his case, though dramatically extreme, may be more typical than it might seem. Action as part of a large group is likely to be at least as problematic as individual choice, and maybe far more common. Unless morality is privatized to the extent that it only relates to matters of the individual and maybe the family, very few important choices are truly individual and very few actions are simple, with simple consequences. Consequently, discussion of simplified examples may be more than misleading. Why, for that matter, do we tend to start our thinking about responsibility from the individual? Could it be in enlightened reaction against some older, more primitive view of communal guilt? Or could it merely be that it is easier?

It is not hard to cut short this whole cloudy discussion with clear, polarized answers. On the one hand, responsibility must always rest in a single, specified point. In this case that point could not be plainer: Truman. The U.S. Constitution determined lines of power and responsibility. In an accurate legal sense, everyone in the Manhattan Project could say that they were responsible to the Commander in Chief. Truman himself accepted that. Paul Tibbetts, commander of the *Enola Gay*, which dropped the bomb on Hiroshima, recalled a meeting with Truman:

> He looked at me for 10 seconds and he didn't say anything. And when he finally did, he said, "What do you think?" I said, "Mr. President, I think I did what I was told." He slapped his hand on the table and said: "You're damn right you did, and I'm the guy who sent you. If anybody gives you a hard time about it, refer them to me."[3]

In a sense of unforced personal choice, each individual in the project (outside the armed forces) had the capacity to decide whether or not to take part. So responsibility, however regarded, lay with individuals. On the other hand—now rather more fashionably—everyone in the project or, even still more widely, in a democratic society, was collectively responsible. For whatever reason, after 1945 the understood scope of guilt or responsibility appears to have widened steadily, to the extent that it can now seem plausible to think about the culpability of whole nations over long periods for colonialism, slavery, genocide, or racism.[4] This can go to strange lengths. It is possible—justifiably or not—for an American born long after 1945 to visit Hiroshima and experience some sense of responsibility for what happened there. German schoolchildren born well after 1945 are still encouraged to visit former concentration camps, presumably in part to cultivate, if not a feeling, then an understanding of some wide sense of responsibility. Hannah Arendt's approach, in 1968, was to deal with "collective responsibility" with an insistence that "guilt, unlike responsibility, always singles out. Where all are guilty, no one is."[5]

Oppenheimer's own view—retrospectively, in 1948—was that "the true responsibility of a scientist, as we all know, is to the integrity and vigor of his research." He was skeptical of the view that "the scientist should assume responsibility for the fruits of his work." He thought that "such assumption of responsibility" had been ineffective in the past and would be "necessarily ineffective" in the future. Far more strongly:

> In fact, it appears little more than an exhortation to the man of learning to be properly uncomfortable; and, in the worst instances, is used as a sort of screen to justify the most casual, unscholarly and, in the last analysis, corrupt intrusion of scientists into other realms of which they have neither experience nor knowledge, nor the patience to obtain it.[6]

Again, the point is not to locate Oppenheimer on some spectrum of responsibility between the legally narrow and the impossibly wide, but to ask what responsibility means. There are many interwoven threads.

❧

First, how far can there be any thought of responsibility outside any context of blame or indictment? We may approve or disapprove of an action, but where there is no framework of judgment, what is the point of our attitude, one way or another? Should we be thinking, two generations later, of understanding rather than judgment? And why should this have been any different in the past? Who are *we*, anyway?

In the latter half of the twentieth century (largely as a result of the work of Donald Davidson), there was a good deal of philosophical discussion on the causality of actions: on the relation between reasons, motives, and causes when an individual performs a voluntary action. There has always been discussion of what makes a person's action genuinely voluntary, and the excuses that can be given by an individual to transfer or mitigate responsibility. But none of this is relevant now. What Oppenheimer did could be subsumed under many descriptions—he directed a research program, led a team of scientists, built bombs, helped to end a war, and so on—and the value of what he did might vary from description to description—this will be a theme of chapter 7—but there could be no point in quibbling over his causal agency in any of them.

Responsibility suggests not only causality but some kind of answerability; but answerability to what, or to whom, if anyone? One initial thought might be that responsibility makes sense within a framework of laws, regulations, morality, understood duties, obligations, relationships, or whatever. You can be responsible *as* a voter, a car driver, a mother, a schoolteacher, a debtor, or an employer. Possibly, you can be responsible *as* a human being, as the pure agent of a deed. But that does not escape the need for some context. Even human beings need to be characterized somehow. On one understanding, a Robinson Crusoe (severely interpreted: before he met Man Friday, and with no strings back at home) could not be responsible to or for anything because there was no framework of society within which he had to answer. Another interpretation—Kant's[7]—would be that responsibility to and for oneself is the most significant kind: but that only seems to illustrate the point that responsibility has to be *to* something, or it would not exist at all.

One framework of understanding might be provided by a narrower reading of culture, tradition, or religion and another, wider, one by a language. In the former case, there can be a reasonable view that a concept of responsibility used to be understood within a context of a culture formed by a traditional set of religious beliefs. Take away the religion and we are left for better (Nietzsche) or worse (Elizabeth Anscombe[8]) with an unsupported morality which may need to be either revalued or rebuttressed. More cautiously, the language of responsibility might be thought to fit with (and hence depend on) other language— of blame, accountability, excuse, ownership. That language would carry a moral load with too much inertia to be shifted: an aspect of Charles Taylor's "inescapable frameworks." In the background might be Hume's view of moral terminology: "Whoever recommends any moral virtues really does no more than is implied by the terms themselves."[9] Either way, the implication might be that responsibility does not (or cannot) make sense without some context that imparts sense to it and that, at the very least, such a context is none too easy to push aside.

Another route toward the same position comes from the thought that asking about responsibility at all must lead to some kind of judgment. If responsibility does imply more than just causality and if the extra element has to be a matter of appraisal, then we cannot ask about responsibility in detachment from assumptions that will be tinged with values or standards. Instead of asking who are we to judge, we might as well ask how we can not judge.

This will seem too strong. Surely there can be understanding (of past human actions) without blame, or, rather, an ascription of responsibility without approval or disapproval? What would pure understanding be like? Historical understanding might seem to offer a suitable example. Beyond a certain time, the element of blame or guilt must surely cease to matter, or matter much less. (A musical called *Napoleon* has been staged. It may be a while before *Hitler* appears.) But is that so? After five hundred years, there are still debates about whether King Richard III was responsible for the death of his nephews, "the Princes in the Tower." Assuming for the sake of argument that no one feels too strongly about this (though some people do, as a matter of fact), it might offer a case of neutral, unjudgmental understanding. But is that so? There are causal questions. Was Richard the direct or indirect cause of the deaths, if they occurred; or did he act to prevent them? Did he know what was happening? Did he intend it to happen? Such factual questions may be settled first. How far does that take us? As far as, for example, a conclusion that he did bring about the death of at least one young kinsman? But is that a neutral judgment or a partial verdict? What would it mean to stop there, with no opinion on the reasons for what happened? The deaths were, if not natural, political assassinations to clear the succession to the throne. Although it is possible to take a Machiavellian line, that the removal of inconvenient relatives was just an expected part of renaissance court behavior, there must be a distinction between an explicit refusal to make an implicit or explicit judgment and a decision that some historical statute of limitation has passed, when judgment is either impossible or inappropriate. The former is itself a moral policy whose basis can be questioned. (It would constitute a decision to abstain not merely from moralizing, but from a thorough statement of reasons, intentions, and motives.) The latter may pose as pragmatic—what is the point of moralizing about the fifteenth century? who cares?—but may be difficult to put into practice. This may be another example where what seems like neutral ground is not so neutral.

The difficulty is not hard to identify. A language of pure understanding is elusive. This is not because historical facts cannot be stripped of all traces of interpretation but because any line drawn between concepts (or uses of language) will be arbitrary. (Hume himself was scarcely a model of neutrality. His paragraph on the episode opens by describing it as "a scene truly tragical, the murder of the two young princes."[10]) We could ask whether Richard was or was not the cause of death of his young nephews. The only conceivable reason why he would have been the cause was one of political ambition or convenience. Already, the step from *what happened* toward *why it happened* is unavoidable. And even the barest account of what happened could scarcely be given: Motivated by a desire for the throne, Richard arranged the secret death of his young nephews. Why secret? Because open killing of children was not acceptable, even by contemporary standards. Could there be a legitimate desire for a throne when a principle of succession should have made ambition irrelevant? We—or sober historians—do not have to praise or condemn, but issues of responsibility must relate to questions of reasons for actions, and then some background of standards—even if they are only local conventions—will be unavoidable. This seems to be confirmed rather than rebutted by one historian's preference for what he sees as implicit rather than explicit judgment:

> Overloading the historian's text with expressions of moral outrage will add little to the argument.
> In making moral judgments on the past, historians have far more powerful rhetorical and stylistic weapons at their disposal than mere denunciation: sarcasm, irony, the juxtaposition of rhetoric and reality, the factual exposure of hypocrisy, self-interest and greed, the uncommented recounting of courageous acts or rebellion and defiance. All of this can be achieved without the direct application of the transient moral vocabulary of the society the historian is living in.[11]

More consistently and severely, when Spinoza declared at the beginning of his *Political Treatise*, "I have taken great care not to deride, bewail, or execrate human actions, but to understand them,"[12] he was distancing himself from praise and blame exactly because his determinism left him with no distinction between the cause and the reason for an action. The price of not judging is a good deal of conceptual pruning.

This may be unsurprising to the point of circularity: matters of responsibility are hard to disconnect from questions of judgment of some kind. To ask how, or how far, Oppenheimer was responsible in the Manhattan Project will lead us to ask what and whose standards in responsibility we have in mind.

Collective action is, by definition, a way of transferring responsibility from the individual to a group. It is easy to forget that a main purpose

of the existence of corporations may be to relocate a burden of responsibility. The whole point of a limited liability company, for example, is to define and restrict the financial responsibilities of
stockholders. At least part of the point of political bodies is to allow
for actions that could not be undertaken by individuals. Similarly,
many types of hierarchy, notably in civil and military services, provide protection for individuals who follow instructions or go along
with decisions within agreed frameworks. A tax official takes responsibility for actions that would be extortion if undertaken by anyone
else. An individual's responsibility as a military officer is necessarily
not the same as a civilian's. That is not some regrettable shortcoming
in military morality or a discordance between private and public behavior. It is a condition without which military action could not be
possible. Most extremely, a state of war alters the powers and responsibilities of the individual in matters of life and death.

Collective or corporate responsibilities provide a framework of
excuses. This does not just mean the classic evasions: I was only
obeying orders; if not me, then someone else. By definition, a state
of war means that in many circumstances it is permissible to kill
while in peace it is not. A particular war may be regarded as illicit,
or the whole concept of war may be repudiated, but as the concept
exists it offers a legitimation for individual actions. In a paradigm
situation, an accepted organization, acting with acceptable means
toward acceptable ends, is joined freely by an individual sharing the
same ends. That situation then, as it were, provides insurance cover
for the individual's actions. Standard examples will be the soldier
fighting freely in a just war justly conducted, or a banker lending
legally in a legal deal. No one imagines that things could ever be so
tidy in real life, but the model seems familiar and convenient.
Complications arise out of deviations from the paradigm: bad gov-
ernments or crooked organizations, bad ends, bad means, forced or
conscripted participation.

The problem is that this simple model can be presented from at
least two conflicting perspectives. Individual conscience may be
weighed against public duty, but from which direction should any
situation be viewed? The historical battle lines are well drawn. From
one angle, the supremacy and freedom of the individual conscience
may be seen as socially determined values. From another angle, communal or organizational virtues of loyalty or solidarity may be seen as
derogations from individual autonomy. Both perspectives may join in

rejecting any notion of a shared or higher morality or legitimacy by which both individual and collective values may be judged.[13]

To concentrate on a question of individual responsibility is to take a view from one of these perspectives. It is to begin from the situation of an individual and then to ask what responsibility meant. The American-European liberal tradition in which Oppenheimer had been raised was one that gave prominence to the place of individual ("conscientious") choice. Principled dissent and individual responsibility would be taken as two sides of the same coin. Just as censure would not be attached to dissent, so an ascription of responsibility could not be withheld from participation. The assumption would be that the individual is free to choose to associate within a group, and to review that association in line with individual values or standards. Excuses that would mitigate the individual's responsibility would themselves be conditional on obligations accepted voluntarily. As a soldier at war you may kill your enemies in uniform. The responsibility for the killing is passed from you to your state; but you are assumed to have accepted, or not repudiated, membership of the state and an association with its chosen means and ends. The responsibility for that acceptance cannot be passed on. There may be a supportive ideology—or mythology—of fortifying stories about heroic dissent motivated by individual conscience.

The trouble with this individualist perspective is its unreality. The Manhattan Project illustrates this well. Oppenheimer's personal contribution was uncontroversially mitigated by his place in a hierarchy that was itself uncontroversially mitigated by its place in a constitutional state. (He himself was ready to take a military commission for the duration of the war, which would have made the position even plainer, but he came to realize that this would never be acceptable to his scientific colleagues.[14]) Any individual, from Roosevelt or Truman through Groves or Oppenheimer to the humblest technician, could have withdrawn from participation (although at least the military personnel would have paid some price for this). All (nonmilitary) individuals, in effect, joined the project voluntarily. But it does not follow at all that responsibility for the project was a straight sum of individual responsibilities.

It is not that a large project takes on a life if its own, obliterating the decisions and responsibilities of those working in it. That would be obviously and dangerously evasive. Here, the complication comes from any idea that individuals could have given continuous assent to

the ends of the Manhattan Project, because those ends altered completely from 1942 to 1945. Truman himself, who accepted responsibility for the use of the first bombs on Hiroshima and Nagasaki, had
no knowledge of the decisions to build the bombs, or of the development work, until after the death of Roosevelt in April 1945. Most of
those who started the work on the bombs had no influence on their
final use. Plainly, anyone who begins working on a government-
sponsored armaments project has to realize that the armaments will
be used as the government chooses. Continuously free, informed participation is a fiction. Responsibility might never be problematic if
every choice really was made independently, one step at a time, free
from the consequences of past choices and unencumbered by the
weight of further choices to come. Problems will arise where fiction
is turned into self-deceiving myth.

Responsibility may imply answerability, if not to an existing court and
code of law then to an implied or assumed court of opinion: we *judge*.
(According to F. H. Bradley, this was essential to what he called "the
vulgar notion of responsibility."[15]) A context of international law and
the concept of a war crime can provide one framework in which
responsibility is apportioned. After 1945, the only major war criminals were on the losing sides. Heisenberg and his colleagues were
treated not as criminals but with more than a little disapproval, even
though their work on atomic weapons had hardly taken shape. (The
treatment of Wernher von Braun makes a disturbing contrast; but his
work was successful, and useful after the war.) If the United States
had somehow been on the losing side in the Second World War, it
is not beyond imagination that Oppenheimer and some of his colleagues might have found themselves on trial. The upshot of that
thought experiment is not merely the cynical view that international
law is determined by the powerful. Blame and responsibility may need
contexts to make clear sense. A court gives the plainest context. A
body of law gives the clearest framework, not only for condemnation
but also for exculpation.

      One conventional view is that morality and law feed off each
other, in both directions. Law has moral roots, in embodying and
codifying the moral sentiments of a community. Morality has been
thought to be lawlike in that it takes account of equity, to an extent

(in the case of Kant) where generality and a judicious fairness may be seen as essential. A context of precedents provides a standard for judgments. So where there is no moral law there will be no morality.

A dissentient view is that morality is importantly different from law: exactly that it is not lawlike. (There is a significant historical angle, connected with the development of Christianity as a nonlaw-based religion, in negative contrast with Judaism.) The analogy between morality and law can be powerfully persuasive. There can be the same language of appraisal, judgment, and blame. There may be analogous approaches through case law or through casuistry, and apparently parallel applications of general principles to particular instances. All this may be significant, but so are the differences. Courts (on the whole) need judges who deliver verdicts. The whole legal apparatus would not be much use if it did not deliver results. (Even a Scottish verdict of "not proven" is a judgment—that evidence may be insufficient to settle a case.) This does not mean that there must always be correct legal decisions, or that legal decisions must be correct; but it does mean that cases get settled conclusively (on the whole, in the end) before an appropriate tribunal. That is in stark contrast with moral issues. The assumption that there must be a right answer, a correct decision, or an appropriate judgment of value is one that can be transposed out of law and into morality without much justification. So may be the assumption that we may position ourselves judicially at all, rather than be satisfied with a position of decision-makers in our own actions and lives. More significant is the role of legal statutes or precedents as models or analogies for moral principles. The presumption in reaching a legal decision may be that there will be some combination of laws and previous cases that will provide either a comparison or general rule. (The young Oliver Wendell Holmes, for one, disagreed, writing that "it is the merit of the common law that it decides the case first and determines the principle afterwards"; but even he went on to say that a series of judicial determinations will permit an induction to the "principle which has until then been obscurely felt."[16]) This may even be true by stipulation in that a court may not be able to hear a case if there is no relevant law.

Understanding morality in lawlike terms can have immediate effects on what is to count as a moral issue. This applies most pointedly, almost as a litmus test, to the ethics of suicide. The very procedure of seeking a verdict on suicide—of making a judgment—leads to a moralistic position, as seen in some of Kant's most prominent examples. In contrast, Hume, following a deliberately Stoic tradition, refused to treat suicide as a matter of morality.[17] A consistent position for him would not be that it was ethically praiseworthy but that moral judgment would not relate to it at all. (And indeed, Hume was scornful of "Philosophers, or rather divines under that disguise, treating all morals as on a like footing with civil laws."[18]) Today, the term "judgmental" is used to imply disapproval. In a different sense, to adopt an attitude of judgment and to seek a framework of guiding principle is to bring suicide within a certain form of morality. (The apt parallel now for suicide in questions of judgment is abortion: in one way seen as deeply immoral, in another as unrelated to morality, perhaps as a matter of "personal choice.")

Conversely, and rather more positively, some choices that might be regarded as ethical can be hard to fit into a morality based on law or lawlike principles. These will include examples favored by admirers of virtue ethics, such as a choice of a career or profession. More widely, in cases when the opposite of praise is not blame but a mere lack of praise, general judgments may only be reached with some strenuous effort. We may admire a schoolteacher who chooses to live and work in a deprived area rather than a comfortable suburb, but no one blames a teacher who does not make that choice, still less anyone who chooses not to become a teacher at all. Nor is this a choice every teacher is obliged to confront. To shrug it off as a matter of supererogation would be to admit that a pattern for morality could not be made to fit.

Chapter 2 looked at Oppenheimer's point of choice—where and how, if anywhere, he could be said to have decided to take the path he did in 1942. A different, and equally elusive point is to ask where responsibility can be attached.

The development of the first atomic bombs is a classic mismatch between intentions and outcomes. Almost all of those who were at Los Alamos at the start of the work in 1942–1943 believed that Germany was likely to develop atomic weapons. Many of them came from Germany and central Europe. Some of them knew Heisenberg, who had refused a position at Columbia as late as 1938, and who had visited America again in 1939, only to return to his work in Germany. Those circumstances alone provided all the reasons they needed for their commitment. At that time, the possible use of atomic weapons seemed distant. If they would be used at all, it would be in Europe, in response to Nazi threat or action. The important aim was to keep step with an unknown menace. By 1945, it was known that there had been no German bomb and by May 1945 the European war was over. No one believed that there was an atomic threat from Japan. The first bombs were used there, for whatever reason, with devastating effects.

By 1945, killing large numbers of civilians without warning from the air was still not universally acceptable as a means of warfare. Before 1945, it was possible to foresee how destructive nuclear weapons would be. Since 1945, the legality of nuclear weapons has been challenged in international courts. The legitimacy of the state was never in doubt, but the legality of its actions might have been. The consequences of a decision taken by Oppenheimer in 1942 were not entirely unpredictable. The initial reluctance of Rabi to take part in the Manhattan Project was based on conscience. Both his non-participation and Oppenheimer's participation may be esteemed or respected, in that both could be grounded in estimable principles. Rabi believed that atomic weapons could and probably would be used, and that any use would be bad. Oppenheimer believed that their use would be decided by a government that had a proper right to take such decisions. With hindsight we may disagree with either prognostication while also accepting that both were made in good faith. An appraisal based on defensible intentions seems to get nowhere.

So for what was Oppenheimer responsible? Not, for sure, the first decision to start the research work. Nor the decision to use the bombs in August 1945. These negative points are much clearer than any positive ones. At a time when Oppenheimer's contribution made an undeniably decisive difference—the enlistment and stimulation of the first research teams in 1943—his intentions could surely only be judged against the background of a potential threat from Germany. He could have abandoned the work in 1944 or 1945 when its likely target shifted, as could many others (and as Rotblat did). Equally, the longer the work went on, the less decisive was the contribution of any single individual. Is there any relevant difference between entering into a commitment and not departing from it when circumstances change? The situation, of course, was not one of theoretical tidiness. Leaving Los Alamos in 1944 would have been imaginable but barely practicable for Oppenheimer. Everything known about him indicates that his commitment never faltered, even when there were serious misgivings among the project's scientists (mainly in Chicago) during the spring of 1945.

In terms of conventional moral philosophy, here is a blunt contrast between the value assigned to intentions before an action and the value of the consequences after it. But the disproportion of the contrast is grotesque. Few would question the motives of the physicists who thought they might be protecting civilization against Hitler. Many have questioned the effects of nuclear physics on Hiroshima and Nagasaki. The harshness of the contrast raises themes mentioned in chapter 2, of moral luck and guilt by association. Mere participation in the Manhattan Project, by planning, research, construction, or execution, might be thought to entail not responsibility but a taint of association. This was, to an extent, a matter of "luck," in that the consequences could not have been foretold when the work started. How can the appraisal of responsibility depend so capriciously not only on the success of an outcome but on such complete unpredictability between intentions and consequences?

One obvious answer is that there is no reason why there should be a single object of judgment. It makes perfectly good sense to say that excellent intentions lead to unforeseen, questionable consequences. That is true, but is does not get us far in thinking about responsibility. In deciding to take on the leadership of atomic research, Oppenheimer was completely responsible for making his own choice. Do we want to say that he was less completely responsible for the consequences of that choice? It is true that responsibility for the consequences was shared, to some degree, in that Truman—the only candidate for sole responsibility—was not even in at the start. But any clear answer looks uneasy. In forming an opinion on Oppenheimer—to sidestep the more forthright notion of judgment—we can say, for the sake of argument, that his intentions may have been praiseworthy, and that for these alone he held responsibility. The actual consequences could not have been predicted, although it might have been reasonable to expect that newly invented weapons in wartime would be used somehow. So complete responsibility one way, partial or mitigated responsibility in another? Again, that sounds reasonable, except for the disproportionate significance of the consequences. Does that matter or not?

It is in utilitarian terms that the clearest verdict can be passed. The only possible consequence of the use of atomic weapons on cities must be the horrible deaths of countless people. Decisions on the use of the first bombs on Japan were framed in utilitarian terms, and they are still defended by the use of the harshest utilitarian

calculations. So many American military deaths in a possible invasion (the "costs" or the "price" in the official discussions[19]) are to be
weighed against so many Japanese civilian deaths as the bombs were
used. To a utilitarian moralist, such a calculation may be convincing
and decisive. It might produce tidy results for decision-makers, but
it cannot pretend to be independent of prior assessments of value:
assessments, for example, that all deaths are to be counted equally,
or that some are more equal than others. These prior assessments
may govern what happens. A weapon has to be evaluated in terms
of its effects, but the accountancy of the consequences may not be
so straightforward. With the atom bomb that was notoriously true,
in that the full consequences of its invention cannot be reckoned
half a century later. Indeed, the uncertainty of outcomes or results
makes utilitarian valuation doubtful for any purpose. It is striking
that bluntly utilitarian calculations actually played so little part in
the political discussions on the use of the bomb before August 1945.[20]
For the scientists at the time of their recruitment to the Manhattan
Project, including Oppenheimer, the consequences of their work
were unpredictable. For whatever reason, it seems undeniable that
there were no serious thoughts or discussions about the political and
international effects of the bomb until the project was effectively
unstoppable. Even if those discussions had started earlier, the world
of 1945 and 1946 was unimaginably different from the world of 1942
and 1943, and it is unlikely that any sensible understanding of the
future could have emerged.

If the possible consequences of the bomb were of little help to
those making decisions on their work in 1942 and 1943, any absolute
moral rule or principle must have seemed even more elusive. There
were many scientists, including Oppenheimer, who may have been
repelled by the use of their work to produce weaponry. But the issue
was never so clear, and nothing is gained by raising it in a simple
form. The Second World War was not much of a time for unqualified
pacifism. Even a limited knowledge of what was happening in Europe
might have been enough to provide some justification for starting the
work at Los Alamos. Plainly, if the circumstances of the use of the
two bombs in August 1945 had been known—or foreseen—in 1943,
many decisions might have been different; but no one can be accused
of undue lack of foresight.

٭٤٥

What follows about appraisal or judgment? What can we say now about responsibility for a decision taken in 1942? What factors should have been appropriate in taking a decision in 1942?

One approach might be loosely legalistic. In courts of law it is not uncommon, of course, to see people who end up doing bad things for, at the outset, the best of reasons. It is not uncommon to see bad consequences arising from lack of foresight or from inability to see the results of actions. If a court has to reach a verdict, it will weigh the seriousness of effects against the extent of caution and foreknowledge, according to well-established rules. It is possible to ask whether some-one could have reasonably predicted the outcome of a choice or ac-tion, and to examine evidence for and against. A context of law provides an understood framework of mitigation. Also, crucially, it provides a context in which some judgment of responsibility is made, within some context of authority, if not legitimacy.

These banal and familiar facts are both relevant and curiously irrelevant. We understand, in *judging* Oppenheimer, what a court can do, to the extent that it is almost impossible not to think in judicial terms. On the one side: guilty—many tens of thousands of deaths. On the other: not guilty—the best of motives, the framework of a legiti-mate state and its decision-making. So, verdict: not guilty—a matter of overwhelming mitigation. It is worth noting why this sounds ab-surdly inappropriate (and not merely because of the blurring between responsibility and guilt). First, of course, because Oppenheimer was not an trial: on the contrary, he received the praise and congratula-tion of his country for his work (at least until 1954). More significantly, there is the absence of any context of legal judgment. In presuming to judge, in the sense of a shadowy thought-experiment of accusation, trial, and acquittal, we do not merely rely on an easy format for reaching an opinion. We assume a position, if not a right, as judges and maybe the possibility of some verdict that will be decisive.

Another approach can lurch to the extreme in the opposite direction: not legalistic but tragic. As not judges but as spectators we can see a man driven by the best of reasons toward a train of action from which he felt unable to escape and that led to consequences that caused him, as he said, "terrible" moral scruples. The emphasis here will be on sympathy rather than direct judgment (though there has to be some implied judgment or we would never be able to summon the required frisson of tragic horror). Interestingly, the emphasis may not be on the attribution of simple causality. This is the terrain of moral luck. It is the "unlucky" association with the dramatic consequences that brings the stigma, without too much fine examination of degrees of participation or mitigation.

Legalistic assumptions rely on the need or desire for a verdict. Conflict between aims and consequences will have to be resolved because some judgment is required. A tragic view relies on exactly the opposite thought, that values or standards may be irreconcilable. Just because our instincts are paradoxical or inconsistent, any decisive conclusion would leave one or another instinct unsatisfied. We want someone to blame, even when there is no one person who can be blamed. We want a man to regard himself as blameless, even though he may suffer from deep remorse. Our own perspective can vary, too. We may judge, or apply criteria that would be used in judgment. We weigh up motives, consequences, degree of participation, mitigation. Yet a tragic perspective does not work unless we can say: that could be me. If there is judgment, there can also be some sense that judgment is inappropriate or intolerable. That sense may go further than a conflict of rules or principles, to a feeling that no rules could apply to a case that seems perversely unique. This applies both to textbook cases of moral luck and to the usual repertory of examples from tragic drama. The case of Oppenheimer might be much less striking if he had been a bloodthirsty monster, longing to try out new weaponry on innocent cities, or a cold technocrat who had gone into his work without a thought on its significance and had left it without a moment's remorse. Possible sympathy may be important for dramatic feeling, but a first step toward it is a sense of particularity. It is not that the more specific a case will be, the greater the difficulty of fitting it into general legal or moral rules. The thought may be exactly that rules are irrelevant.

A conflict of perspectives can be explained from a historical angle. We are heirs—both to an older view of the individual as the owner of the deed, bound to it by fate as much as by causality, and to a more modern, bureaucratized understanding of responsibility defined and assessed by rational, legal rules. It should not be surprising that we can be confused, since one perspective is inconsistent with the other. Perhaps we should prefer to be modern, while recognizing that a less tidy mentality is not so easy to suppress. The *should* in the previous sentence reveals the catch in such historical relativism. No doubt our opinions do have different, inconsistent origins. Yet we can still ask which we should hold.

Along similar lines it is possible to argue that responsibility was once seen as communal or collective, where the tribe or social group shared the onus and would expect to be rewarded or punished together. Individual, personal responsibility may have been a later development.[21] Whether or not that speculative history is accurate, it hardly follows that the allegedly newer view should supersede the older as better, nor that we have a neutral choice of perspectives to be selected according to taste. If it is true that we have conflicting understandings of responsibility, then a knowledge of history does nothing to remove the need to remove or reduce that conflict. Nor does it imply that any conflict is irremovable.

In the case of Oppenheimer, the reasons for ambivalence are not difficult to see. Taking a purely individualistic view of his personal contribution—of his choice to work and continue working at Los Alamos—he was responsible for his own decisions and was responsible as the appointed leader of a project. The outcome of the project was the destruction of two cities and the birth of nuclear weapons, with consequences still too large to be estimated. The most rigid view of hierarchical responsibility does indeed tie together the responsibility of the individual with responsibility for the consequences of collective action. That is not so much the statement of a problem as it is one possible solution.

To assign responsibility is to make a judgment, to reach a verdict. For a legitimate state operating legitimately, questions of blame or guilt should not even arise. Responsibility is rationalized and blame is inappropriate. A framework of legitimacy—more literally, of law—should clarify questions of responsibility completely, in its own terms. This is an optimistic moral from the *Eumenides* of Aeschylus, in which the terrible pollution of matricide is balanced by the justice of Athene. The Furies, with their devotion to ancient rules of blood, end up housed in a well-appointed temple, flattered but tamed. The problem, as the drama leaves uncomfortably obvious, lies in believing that this is the end of the story.

❧

A further sense of "responsibility" is where its opposite is "irresponsibility," when "acting responsibly" suggests considered care. (This itself suggests a significant theme in the history of atomic weapons and atomic power that will appear explicitly in the next chapter, on the idea that the development of atomic weapons was an unprecedented and irreversible step.) In fact, there may not be a double sense in responsibility at all. Ownership of an action and liability to answer for it are not be unconnected with a notion of due care. If to be responsible is to be answerable in more than a merely causal sense, then being responsible and acting responsibly may not be far apart.

Levinas—once again at odds with mainstream moral philosophy—regarded responsibility—understood as regard and care for "the other"—as ethically fundamental. He believed that the rhetorical challenge in the question "Am I my brother's keeper?" was based on assumptions, which he repudiated, that the self cares first about itself, and that concern for others, whether directly, through sympathy, or less directly, through a theory of social contract, was derivative. Instead, the identity of the individual was to be defined in relation to others. The relationship was one of responsibility, to the point of what he called substitution. So responsible action—as concern for others—would not stand in need of further justification. It would be essential to personal identity.[22] This line of thinking might be expected to appeal against a background in which individual concern had been eroded—as in wartime imprisonment in the case of Levinas or under ideological oppression in the case of Václav Havel, one of his most interesting admirers, who wrote:

> To a certain extent, our actions are always illuminated by responsibility. What this means is that we can always justify them in some way, defend them in advance, stand behind them, own up to them, identify with them, consider them correct or, if not correct, then at least come to terms with that . . . Yes, a boundless and unmotivated sense of responsibility, that "existence beyond our own existence," is undoubtedly one of the things into which we are primordially thrown and which constitutes us.[23]

For now, the validity of this perspective is less significant than what it shows about the relevance of a starting-point. Where there is a need to reinforce a damaged sense of individual accountability, the individual ownership of actions may seem to matter first. Identity may be established as autonomy. The position of Oppenheimer, in a society that placed the greatest emphasis on unconstrained individual choice, was diametrically different. No one would disagree that is was

up to him to decide what to do, or that—in a sense all too recognizable from its denial in a totalitarian society—his choice was free. His
situation, and the problem it created, was not one of establishing
autonomy, but of how far autonomy was lost or submerged in collective action freely undertaken. Deciding *not to* join a collaborative
project—to dissent—clarifies and fosters readily identifiable, autonomous responsibility. The individual is a recognizable hero. Deciding *to*
join may be to take a share in some degree of responsibility. That
need not be viewed negatively, as a resignation of individual freedom,
just as, at the end of chapter 1, *having no choice* was read positively,
in a sense of an acceptance of responsibility rather than as a denial
of alternatives. In a Protestant tradition, dissent may seem more admirable than cooperation, submission, or obedience. There, the alternatives are not framed impartially. From another angle, cooperation
may imply virtues and duties of acceptance or participation that make
no sense in isolation.

The reality may well be that judgment is too easy, not too difficult.
With hindsight it is easy enough to debate effects and consequences,
even though the outcome of such calculations may change from one
time to another. An apportionment of responsibility may not be
obscure, either within a transparent hierarchy or within a looser system of association. Less clear is the gap between a decision in the past
and a judgment on it later. Our difficulty now is neither one of judging nor of deciding for whatever reason not to judge. It may be one
of seeing that our judgments now are so distinct from a decision in the
past. In the winter of 1942–1943, Oppenheimer took on responsibility
for leading research into an atomic bomb. His share in the success of
the research can be assessed, whether controversially or not. His decision at the time—his judgment to act—was incomparably distant
from any judgment afterward, including his own. Obviously, some of
the facts at the time were uncertain and the future consequences
could not be known. That sounds trite: with good will, you can do
your best in the light of what you know; you can always ask yourself
how posterity will judge you and, if the results turn out badly, that
may be partly your fault, or not. But to act responsibly may be to
accept responsibility for—ownership of—consequences, even though
you cannot know what they can be. The lack of symmetry between

the present and the retrospective is important. Deciding to act as you would wish to be judged, impartially, in the future may be more of a contradiction than a useful fiction. What may be significant about the present decision is exactly that the way in which it is judged subsequently may be unforeseeable. A decision and a judgment cannot be the same. Decisions may be necessary; judgment maybe not.

CHAPTER SIX

IRREVERSIBLE CHANGE

Henry L. Stimson, Secretary of War, wrote in a memorandum to Truman on September 11, 1945:

> If the atomic bomb were merely another though more devastating military weapon to be assimilated into our pattern of international relations, it would be one thing. We could then follow the old custom of secrecy and nationalistic military superiority relying on international caution to prescribe the future use of the weapon as we did with gas. But I think the bomb instead constitutes merely a first step in a new control by man over the forces of nature too revolutionary and dangerous to fit into the old concepts.

More laconically, Groves noted in his memoirs that "there has never been an improvement in weapons comparable in degree and in sudden impact to the atomic bomb."[1]

The feeling that the world had entered a new era in 1945 was immediate and widespread. The political implications were evident. One country—for a time—would possess devastating military superiority. Few believed that this could last. In the 1950s there followed international debates about the Cold War balance of terror and extensive discussion, at all levels of sophistication, about the morality of nuclear weapons.[2]

This chapter is about the first step into that new era, and its significance. How far can we be justified in thinking that the atomic bomb represented something either unprecedented or irreversible—or perhaps unprecedented *because* it was irreversible? What is particularly important about irreversibility anyway? These questions matter because of their particular bearing on scientific development, or, more specifically, on cognitive growth. Scientific knowledge in the modern world has been uniquely cumulative. "There is something irreversible about acquiring knowledge," wrote Oppenheimer in 1948.[3] For realistic purposes, what has been discovered cannot be undiscovered. Knowledge may be hard to obtain; but a movement from a state of knowledge back to a state of ignorance is even harder to achieve.

What does this imply? The most obvious thought—simply *be careful*—can be alarmingly irrelevant. Some of the thinking reviewed in chapter 4 might suggest that knowledge—truth—research must be pursued. Even more strongly, there is the thought that we do not really know how to frame the very idea of a research program that is not based on an unqualified pursuit of truth. So caution seems irrelevant almost by definition. Possible consequences, however great, seem detachable from the purity of the pursuit of knowledge. One solution has been reliance on a distinction between pure and applied research (and the importance of this will be considered in the next chapter). From a practical point of view, that might have some relevance. Knowledge of how to make atomic weapons is effectively irreversible, short of some entirely overwhelming global catastrophe. Technical capacity to make atomic weapons might be less so.[4] It is possible to imagine the industrialized world meeting a reversal comparable to the ending of the Roman Empire, so that the technology required to purify uranium, for example, might be no more attainable than the construction of Roman central heating in tenth-century England. But this is far-fetched.

In terms of a utilitarian body-count, it is often pointed out that Hiroshima and Nagasaki were outstripped, even in the same war. The firebombing of Tokyo in March 1945, and certainly the programs of industrialized killing in Europe, were far more destructive. Taking into account the lives said to be saved by the first use of atomic weapons, the accounting balance might even be thought to be positive. Even so, there are two main reasons for a concentration on the invention of atomic weapons, one more often emphasized than the other. There was the evident potential for further, still more destructive, development. "It was indeed the bizarre nature of the bomb, and the uncanny nature of the future it suggested, rather than its actual results in the war, that impressed people," wrote Vannevar Bush in 1950.[5] Those who lobbied against the construction of the hydrogen bomb—including Oppenheimer, to his later personal cost—were aware of how much more terrible weapons might become. It was not apparent in the early 1940s that the wholesale destruction of all life on the planet was a possibility, but this did not take long to emerge. Atomic weapons turned out to be unprecedented in their potential for harm, gigantically out of proportion to anything before. A second factor is just the irreversibility of their development. Not only was their further development hard to control—a result of the curiosity debated in chapter 4—but their invention could not be reversed; they could hardly be uninvented. Firebombs, gas chambers, and *Blitzkrieg* may have become industrialized extensions of conventional means of death.[6] Atomic bombs were the outcome not only of technology and industry but also of a science that developed when it did and at no other time. The knowledge on which they were based was new, and was not going to go away. As Oppenheimer commented, for physicists, "this is a knowledge which they cannot lose." His much-criticized allusion to "sin"[7] was not a comment on the contamination of science by immersion in the arms business as much as on the one-way change for which he had assumed responsibility. Pandora's box, once opened, would not shut again. That imagery, though almost unavoidable, may not be wholly appropriate. The mythology of a dangerous, irreversible discovery is ancient and so—presumably—the issues surrounding such discoveries must have been well rehearsed. Yet the challenge created at Los Alamos seemed to be of something *new*, not a familiar story in modern dress. Victor Weisskopf thought of "a new form of scientific life"; "Physics, science and human society were different after the nuclear explosion in Alamogordo." Mary McCarthy wrote that it was in the moral world that the atom bomb exploded.[8] How right is it to think in terms of some moral difference, as though the world for us really had changed on July 16, 1945, at 5.30 a.m.? More to the point, what is gained, apart from rhetorical force, in thinking about new or unprecedented moral categories?

To begin, there is a utilitarian, statistical calculation about the scale of damage. From the start it was recognized that atomic weapons had a capacity to kill large numbers of people, to the extent that discrimination between military and nonmilitary victims had become irrelevant. Before too long it was recognized that nuclear weapons could cause enough destruction to wipe out civilizations, or even the whole of human life on Earth. On a less apocalyptic scale, the long-term damage caused by radiation was effectively unmeasurable. There could be biological consequences, to an unknown extent, into a future far longer than previous human history.

The utilitarian balance is straightforward. The potential consequences of atomic weapons are so great, so long term, and so irreversible as to be beyond measurement. They can be considered as unlimited, insofar as no one can know the extent of genetic alterations over a long period, and insofar as contamination for thousands of years into the future has no meaning in terms of current history. As early as 1940, in a preliminary memorandum "On the construction of a 'Super-bomb'; based on a Nuclear Chain Reaction in Uranium," Otto Frisch and Rudolf Peierls had noted that "the radiations would be fatal to human beings even a long time after the explosion."[9] At the time of the first atomic test there was still reckoned to be a remote possibility that a catastrophic chain reaction might destroy literally everything. The calculation—reminiscent of Pascal's wager—might be that unknowably large future effects must outweigh any other present considerations. Whatever the immediate benefits from the development or use of atomic weapons, these could never outweigh the potentially open-ended effects of their use. The moral innovation, in these terms, would lie in the notion of unlimited future harm that would counterbalance any current good.

The first, very obvious drawback with such a calculation would be in where or when it might have been used, and by whom. Today, we may judge that the invention of atomic weapons has had arguably good or bad effects since 1945, to be balanced against unmeasurably bad possible future effects. That retrospective utilitarian reckoning is clear in outline but unhelpful to the point of uselessness. What are we judging—What should have happened? What someone should have done or not done? But who, in reality? For the scientists going to Los Alamos in 1943, the issue was not so much the first invention of atomic weapons, but the Allies' capacity to use them if they were first developed in Germany. By 1945, the issue for Roosevelt and then Truman may have been the use of the atom bomb in relation to its unavoidable development by the Soviet Union: As Blackett put it in 1948, "not so much the last military act of the second world war, as the first act of the cold diplomatic war with Russia now in progress."[10] In any event, the rightness of the use of the bomb is not the same question as the estimation of the consequences of its invention. This is not a mere quibble, as Oppenheimer himself acknowledged ruefully:

GRAY: Then may I ask you this: Do you make a sharp distinction between the development of a weapon and the commitment to use it?

OPPENHEIMER: I think there is a sharp distinction but in fact we have not made it.[11]

If there was some moral sea change in 1945, it was surely at the time of the Trinity test, when the destructive capacity of the bomb became certain, rather than at Hiroshima, when its effects were appalling but not, regrettably, entirely unprecedented. Hamburg and Tokyo—or Troy and Carthage—were destroyed just as thoroughly as Hiroshima and Nagasaki. It was the possible future use of atomic weapons, at least as much as their actual use, that seemed dismaying.

If it is felt that anyone at the time could or should have performed some utilitarian calculation, the scientists working in the German atomic program might have been the appropriate candidates. They "could" have calculated that the potential effects of their work would be too devastating for it to continue. They could have refused openly, and could have made this known, to the extent that the work at Los Alamos could have become unnecessary. Such a scenario only needs to be sketched for its implausibility to be evident.

In Oppenheimer's case, personally, he could have judged that the outcome of atomic research might be so bad as to overbalance any potential good, whatever the situation in Germany, and he could have played no further part. A utilitarian Oppenheimer might have reckoned in 1942 that his role would make the difference between failure and success, or between earlier and later success. He might have been right if he had judged in 1942 that only his leadership would enable the bomb to be ready in time to be used by August 1945; but again, that just needs to be stated to be seen as meaningless. Again, the artificiality of those suppositions should surely give a hint that the whole framework is fanciful (and, as seen in chapter 2, the point at which he might have made any such choice is quite unclear). Any scientist could have taken the view that it was wrong to work toward the production of armaments, of course. There could be a further view—surely indefensible—that it would be more wrong to work on large, new armaments than on small, old ones. But, either

way, these would hardly be "new" considerations. Oppenheimer used
his talents on behalf of the military power of the United States just
as Leonardo did for the Milanese and Archimedes did for the
Syracusans. There was no difference in principle.

All this indicates the difficulty in the idea that atomic weapons
were morally unprecedented just because of the disproportionate scale
of their potential effects. In that sense, any "moral problem" has to be
entirely retrospective. We can reach a verdict if we wish, but our judgment cannot coincide with any decision taken by anyone relevant at
the time. One utilitarian factor in the bombing of Hiroshima and
Nagasaki—to save lives in the planned invasion of Japan—seems to
have been more prominent as a justification afterward than as an argument before. This, of course, is historically controversial, but it looks
like ironic confirmation that utilitarian arguments run better backward.[12]

This sounds like a desperately negative, fatalist point. It can be
sharpened further by taking a different example: the "Scientists'
Movement" in the United States after 1945, broadly protesting against
the further development of atomic weapons and in favor of international controls or restraint. Surely, it seems that after the immediate
crisis of war, and outside the bounds of civil discipline which it im-
posed—individual scientists were altogether free to withhold their
contributions to further development, taking the view that atomic
weapons had shown themselves to have wholly unprecedented effects.
Much of the rhetoric of that time centered on the need for new moral
and political frameworks to deal with new military power. Was this
not a recognition of a new moral world, based on a new reality of
unlimited possible harm?

It may have been, but some practical factors are unfortunately
relevant. The scientists who were active in opposing the extension of
nuclear research after 1945 were, archetypally, shutting the stable
door after the horse had vanished. It would have required greater—
unlikely—unanimity to have prevented any further developments. The
potential damage—the knowledge of how to make atomic weapons—
was already in existence. That could not be wished away. Further, as
the scientists knew only too well, by 1945, serious questions were out
of their hands. The president's military advisors had no intention of
restraining research, or of sharing knowledge internationally, or of
allowing substantial international controls.[13] This was not a new moral
world at all, but an assumption of political and military power that
Machiavelli would have easily recognized.

A second general drawback in a notion of unlimited possible future harm is familiar from many critiques of utilitarianism. There are innumerable cases in which known, present good or evil has to be balanced against open-ended, unquantifiable, future consequences. Zhou En Lai's famous remark that it is too early to evaluate the French Revolution gives the clearest illustration. At the time of a decision (and for long afterward) it may be unrealistic to assess future consequences. A large political change—a revolution, an assassination, an election—will have unforeseen effects. This can support a Burkean, conservative case against abrupt change. Alternatively, it can be taken as a refutation of a utilitarian reckoning of consequences. In political terms, that may make sense. Nothing would ever happen if allowance had to be made for unpredictable effects. In many circumstances, the choice of doing nothing may not exist.

That point may be less impressive in scientific matters, when consequences may be exactly quantifiable and when a decision not to proceed—to do nothing—may be realistic. During the period of enthusiasm for nuclear power, from the 1950s to the 1980s, for example, it was predictable that by-products and waste would be active for millennia, creating a massive problem for posterity. That problem might appear to be so long term as to be open-ended in terms of current history, outweighing any present gains. This would seem like a classic utilitarian case of the kind now under discussion. In those terms, the rapid development of nuclear power could be seen as a prime exemplar of scientific irresponsibility. A contrary view might also be utilitarian: that half-lives and nuclear risks are not in fact open-ended, but precisely quantifiable, allowing for a finite balance of present utilities against future disutilities. One general conclusion might be that a "new" morality comes into play—or at least an old one ceases to operate—when sums cannot be done. But that seems barely plausible. Nuclear power programs have been stalled or reversed in many countries exactly because open-ended risks are now seen to outweigh current gains. This has come out in terms of financial, insurance liability when power plants are privately owned or in terms of possible environmental damage when public pressure has had a part to play. Once more, this has not been the advent of a new moral era as much as an older, possibly unsatisfactory form of moral accountancy catching up with a new technology. The same could happen with nuclear weapons, though there are obvious reasons why it may not.

None of this is to belittle the scale of what was done at Hiroshima and Nagasaki. The destruction was terrible, but it was not this alone that provoked thoughts of a wholly new era, maybe with a need for some new morality. Already, earlier in the same war, the sudden destruction of cities had become taken for granted as part of warfare.[14] The bombing of Hiroshima and Nagasaki could have been the end point from that numbing of sensibilities. Also, there was considerable talk of revenge for Pearl Harbor. (White House press release, August 6, 1945: "The Japanese began the war from the air at Pearl Harbor. They have been repaid many fold."[15]) Both points of view would represent the reverse of a moral revolution; rather, the outcome from some ancient views of retaliation or revenge. One thought, though, could be that such conventional calculations were wholly out of place in a transformed situation.

The Manhattan Project is often seen as the origin of what came to be known—mostly by its critics—as the scientific–military–industrial complex. Until then, so it might be thought, pure science and impure military force could be kept separate, at least to the extent that scientists did not need to dwell too long on the potentially military outcomes of their research. So new questions of engagement and commitment were raised. As Habermas put it in one of his early reflections on "technocracy":

> To the extent that the sciences are really taken into the service of political practice, scientists are objectively compelled to go beyond the technical recommendations that they produce and reflect upon their practical consequences. This was especially and dramatically true for the atomic physicists involved in the production of the atomic and hydrogen bombs.[16]

Yet the fact that discoveries, theoretical or not, may have dramatic and unforeseen consequences was scarcely new. A distinction between pure and applied science, or technology, will be discussed in the next chapter. It cannot be brought in here with any conviction. The step from the "pure" equivalence of mass and energy to the harsh reality of the explosion at Alamogordo may have seemed unusually abrupt, but it may not have been unprecedented. Archimedes is supposed to have used his knowledge of optics to help the defense of Syracuse, and so on through history.

On the other hand, as the White House press release went on:

the greatest marvel is not the size of the enterprise, its secrecy, nor its cost, but the achievement of scientific brains in putting together infinitely complex pieces of knowledge held by many men in different fields of science into a workable plan. . . . What has been done is the greatest achievement of organized science in history.[17]

This claim may well have been justifiable. Previous military actions may have been helped by superior knowledge, but the support had seldom been so explicit. Theoretical physics from the twentieth century was a necessary condition for the atomic bomb. The link was all the starker because the first application of atomic physics that was intelligible to most people was the destruction of Hiroshima. The corollary for physicists was not hard for them to see. The purest of theories, and the purest of theorists, were implicated in what had been done—as Einstein, for one, felt strongly; though of course, as seen in the previous chapter, questions of real responsibility were far more complicated.

Despite reservations about historical precedents, the step from apparently theoretical physics to overtly practical weaponry seems unusually striking at Los Alamos. Physicists who had begun their careers only a few years earlier with no thought of warfare found themselves invited to contribute to the largest military program in history. A decade earlier, it would have seemed far-fetched to suggest that research in nuclear physics might ever pose hard choices. Only five years before Hiroshima, and at a time when number theorists were already deeply immersed in military cryptography, G. H. Hardy wrote that "real mathematics has no effect on war. No one has yet discovered any warlike purpose to be served by the theory of numbers or relativity, and it is very unlikely that anyone will do so for many years."[18]

A prosaic reason to think of moral innovation comes just from this sudden change. The assumptions that guide a life in abstract research may not be those that are required in dealing with unprecedentedly powerful weaponry, especially when the change takes place so quickly. For the wider public, the total secrecy of the Manhattan Project made the issues raised by Hiroshima a complete shock. For politicians, it was depressingly clear that new ways of thinking did not match new forms of weaponry. Churchill, for example, was ready with fine words: "This revelation of the secrets of nature, long mercifully withheld from

man, should arouse the most solemn reflections in the mind and conscience of every human being capable of comprehension," although his
private thoughts were less exalted: "I shall certainly continue to urge
the President not to make or permit the slightest disclosure to France
or Russia. Even six months will make a difference should it come to a
show-down with Russia, or indeed with de Gaulle."[19]

It was only too easy to hold on to conventional notions of security and domination. In 1945, that seemed possible. Later, in the
1960s, a different consideration came to the fore in debates over
the uniqueness of nuclear weapons: that they were unusable in practice. Just after Hiroshima and Nagasaki, and before the days of vast
nuclear stockpiles, this was only a distant prospect.

The sheer scale of atomic weapons and the direct role played by atomic
physicists may both have seemed revolutionary in 1945. So far in this
chapter, the case has been that neither set the terms for a moral revolution in a sense in which existing tools of thought lost their grip. On
the contrary, the advocacy deployed by the scientists' movement after
1945 relied on entirely familiar arguments and on rhetoric which sprang
readily to hand—as indeed did the opposing pressure of realpolitik from
the State Department (and, presumably, within the Kremlin). A new
moral era may not have come into being.

A rather different thought is that maybe it *should* have. There
does not have to be any single new reason for this, but one factor that
can be persuasive is just the irreversibility of discovery. Atomic weapons depended to a startling degree on not only new technology but
new science. This again, of course, was not unprecedented. Bronze,
iron, steel, the long-bow, gunpowder, and the steamship were all no
doubt inventions of the greatest military significance. Whole eras of
military supremacy may have been founded on technical superiority.
Yet, as the White House press release of August 1945 boasted, what
was remarkable about the Manhattan Project was "the achievement
of scientific brains in putting together infinitely complex pieces of
knowledge held by many men in different fields of science into a
workable plan": an orderly, managed creation of new knowledge, and
its immediate transmutation into new technology, on an industrial
scale. However much that was new, it certainly laid a pattern for the
large-scale exploitation of science after 1945. If there was anything

different direction, the value in being alive can be related to a degree of being alive, in a way that would not have been available when there was no uncertainty between life and death. Then, a tenuous, twilit life may be valued less highly than a full, healthy life (or not, of course). In blunt terms, a new fact—a kind of partial life—may suggest a changed value, or an altogether new value, in being partly alive. Medical discoveries may seem to create clear needs, for new attitudes and choices, that may appear abruptly and (to some extent) irreversibly. At any rate, past certainties may be eroded. This is the case argued by Peter Singer in *Rethinking Life and Death*.[20]

The invention, and then the first use, of the atomic bomb seemed like this at the time. The scientists who started to organize themselves politically from the spring of 1945 saw how the world would change. Because physics was so international, it was futile to imagine that previous notions of secrecy would have any force. What had been discovered at Los Alamos would be discovered elsewhere. For the first time there would be devastating weapons against which there could be no secure defense. To many, it seemed to follow that international cooperation would become unavoidable. Nationalistic attachments would have to wane. Atomic weapons made any distinction between combatants and noncombatants meaningless, to the extent that civilian interest and engagement in warfare could no longer be kept at the margins of political decision-making.

Again, to many, all of this did add up to a reappraisal of values. Secrecy, national assertiveness, and autonomy had to be rethought. The creation, establishment and legitimation of values are controversial. If (for example) tradition is seen as providing both a source and legitimation for value, then "new" values seem problematic. Evolution may be acceptable, but revolution may not. The same applies when value is seen as infused in some direct way from a prevailing social context. Critics of Nietzsche have argued that the wholesale revaluation of values he proclaimed in the *Twilight of the Idols* and the *Antichrist* could have been no more than a repudiation of values that he did not like—associated by him with bourgeois nineteenth-century herd Christianity—in favor of heroic, individual values more to his taste. Not only were the "new" values in fact rather old, but the framework of repudiation and revaluation itself had to be a generally moral one, as would be any suggestion about how one *ought* to act (leaving the suspicion that the despised Kant had been kicked ostentatiously out of the front door only to creep in again at the back).

revelatory about the work on the atomic bomb, it could have
the realization of how immediately science could change the

If there is anything specific to scientific ethics—or if t
such a thing at all—it could be that new knowledge may con
being (and will not go away) with unforeseeable effects on e:
values or codes of judgment. Maybe that seems to beg too
questions: not just a dependence of values on facts—a general t
in chapter 3—but some kind of functionalist dependence: new
call for, or generate, new values. On the contrary, one might feel
matters of value ought to be independent of transitory taste or s
change. Chivalry in warfare, for example, might seem so ov
embedded in a specific (and defunct) social structure that it m
qualify only as a form of etiquette rather than value. As society
technology change, *manners* change with them; but *values*—real, mo
values—should not. A new invention—aerial bombardment, a
common example—may lead a society to rethink some of its rules
conventions—in this case, on the arbitrary killing of noncombatan
But any such revisions would be undertaken in the light of underlyir
(or overarching) morality: prohibitions on random cruelty, th
justification of means and ends and the proportionate use of force. W
are able to make decisions about the use of new weaponry just as fa
as it can be brought within the ambit of existing principles. All of
that could be right but uninformative. Perhaps our framework of judgments—our moral language—can be stretched indefinitely, but without fitting comfortably. The question that must be interesting is
whether there can be genuine innovation that calls for a genuine
renewal or overhaul in how we think or should think.

This can seem most convincing with biological and medical
changes over the past half-century. In 1950, the lines between killing,
saving life and keeping alive may still have been reasonably
uncontroversial. Now, as then, we may be unanimous that killing is
wrong and that saving life is praiseworthy, but we may be less certain
about the boundaries between life and death. How far do new facts
call for new values? It is possible to hold on to a dogmatic definition
of life—to insist on the absolute necessity of preserving it at all cost.
Or it is possible to retain some more general principle—a need to
conserve worthwhile life as far as practicable—that may lead to vary-
ing outcomes as medical capacities develop. One can refuse to admit
that new facts can alter anything, or one can try to adapt existing
principles to accommodate new facts. More radically, and from a

What matters here is not merely a question about moral theory. The questions posed by the atomic bomb now seem as though they should have been predictable. Suppose—one might have asked in 1935—there could be a new weapon against which there could be no defense, which could destroy cities. What would be the effects on international relations? Hence, Oppenheimer could surely have asked himself such questions, as could all of those who launched the Manhattan Project. To some degree, this must have happened. After all, the project started because no one found it hard to imagine what Hitler might do with overwhelming force. Nevertheless, it is striking that the scientists working on the bomb gave remarkably little thought to the wider implications of its use until, in practice, the work had gone so far that few individuals could have stalled it. In 1954, Hans Bethe was asked:

MARKS: . . . what views did the scientists have about the moral or humane problems that many people have discerned in the atomic bomb program at Los Alamos.

BETHE: I am unhappy to admit that during the war—at least—I did not pay much attention to this. We had a job to do and a very hard one. The first thing we wanted to do was to get the job done. It seemed to us most important to contribute to victory in the way we could. Only when our labors were finally completed when the bomb dropped on Japan, only then or a little bit before then maybe, did we start thinking about the moral implications.

John von Neumann was equally candid:

> . . . of course we were all little children with respect to the situation which had developed, namely, that we suddenly were dealing with something with which one could blow up the world. . . . This was a very peculiar situation. None of us had been educated or conditioned to exist in this situation, and we had to make our rationalization and our code of conduct as we went along.
>
> For some people it took two months, for some two years, and for some one year. I am quite sure that all of us by now have developed the necessary code of ethics.[21]

Differing conclusions could be drawn. The physicists might have thought there was no point in worrying about the effects of the bomb until they knew whether it was going to work. The extreme pressure may have left them no time for reflection. There could also be a harsh verdict that they were culpably irresponsible, either out of scientific recklessness or because of some desire to leave the thinking to politicians. There could have been some deficit in imagination, cured instantly by the light of the bomb at Alamogordo. Oppenheimer's blunt remark from 1945 was quoted in chapter 3: "There are people who say that they are not such very bad weapons. Before the New Mexico test we sometimes said that too. . . . After the test we did not say it any more."[22]

◆⑤

An even more unsettling conclusion could be that a problem foreseen is not the same as a judgment in retrospect, and both are crucially different from a problem at a time when, later, we might think it should have been faced. This could go beyond the obvious difference between a possibility and a reality. Truman's manner changed at Potsdam after he got news of the Trinity test. He was "evidently much fortified," Churchill reported, and he "stood up to the Russians in a most emphatic and decisive manner." There was a change in Oppenheimer, too, as Rabi noted: "And he came to where we were in the headquarters . . . and his walk was like "High Noon"—I think it's the best I could describe it—this kind of strut. He'd done it."[23]

Hume diagnosed some of the psychology: "It is not conceivable, how a *real* sentiment or passion can ever arise from a known *imaginary* interest."[24] But there may also be a more fundamental point. What Oppenheimer could have envisaged in 1942 can be seen as what he should have envisaged—at least to the degree that foresight may be a virtue. What was problematic was always going to be problematic, and afterward always was problematic. Failure to see this can be mitigated in many ways, but the starting-point for judgment will be that it should not matter when a moral problem is posed. This comes out in the apologetic tone of the remarks quoted from Bethe and von Neumann. What was seen afterward could, and so should, have been seen before. Kant put one underlying thought in characteristically abstract terms: "reason, when it is a question of the law of our intelligible existence (the moral law) recognizes no distinction of time and asks only whether the event belongs to me as a deed and, if it does, then always connects the same feeling with it morally, whether it was done just now or long ago."[25] Part of the difficulty with this is one of identity, touched on in chapter 2. The exclusion of time from judgment relies on a strong condition that other things are equal. The moral force in "I ought to do x" can be taken as identical with the force in "I ought to have done x," or "I ought to do x next week" (or "you ought to do x," and so on) only where there are no relevant differences between now and then (or between you and me). The strength and significance of that condition are debatable. One can agree, for example, that other things (or, rather, times) can never be exactly equal, but that the condition can have some regulative value that is necessary if moral obligation is to be meaningful at all. Alternatively, there is the argument that counterfactual conditions, even with only some regulative force, remove the whole sense of uncertainty that makes problems problematic. Oppenheimer could have wished that he had known in 1942 what he knew by 1945 about the effects of atomic weapons, and had known by 1950 about their wider influence. He might have accepted that he could have predicted in 1942 what would have happened by 1945 or 1950, although the sense of all these conditionals is not clear. On the other hand, it is reasonable to point out that one factor was neither known nor predictable in 1942—the state of the Nazi bomb project—and this made all the difference. In 1942, if it had been known that the work in Germany was never going to succeed, the Manhattan Project might never have got under way, or might have lacked the drive that kept it going. (It is this counterfactual speculation that has made the meeting in 1941 between Heisenberg and Bohr such an intriguing subject for dramatic fiction, as in Michael Frayn's Copenhagen.) In Oppenheimer's case, such considerations actually may have led to both positive and negative conclusions that he did reach in practice: that he should work on the atomic bomb from 1942, but that he should argue against the immediate development of the hydrogen bomb after 1945.[26] Other things were not at all equal. It does not follow without further argument that any decision has to be, as it were, dated; but it does follow that the use of hypothetical generalization has to be treated with some care. As pointed out in chapter 2, to ask what someone else at the same time in the same situation could or should have done may just be empty.

In the background there may be arguments at cross-purposes. In one direction, it can be argued that, when and if moral obligation does apply, there has to be some sense in which it has a potentially universalized application. (Nagel: "The first step on the path to ethics is the admission of *generality* in practical judgments."[27]) This may be presented as a fact about the "concept" of obligation, rather than as an observation from specific cases. In the other direction, the very point of many hard problems may be that they seem so specific to person, place, and time that to frame them in terms of anyone else, somewhere else, at another time seems just pointless. Disagreement may hinge on whether a concept of moral obligation is a necessary presupposition, is of purely regulative value, or is a worthless abstraction. It is possible to agree that moral obligation does possess some ("logical") properties while denying that it is applicable in a particular case (or in many cases at all, in the view of some critics[28]). Interestingly, Oppenheimer, cross-questioned at the 1954 hearings, was asked about his "opposition to the production of the hydrogen bomb on moral grounds":

ROBB: You had moral qualms about it, is that accurate?

OPPENHEIMER: Let us leave the word "moral" out of it.

ROBB: You had qualms about it.

OPPENHEIMER: How could one not have qualms about it? I know no one who doesn't have qualms about it.[29]

The last chapter ended with the thought that there may be a significant difference between a decision and a retrospective judgment. Kant's notion that the moral law "recognizes no distinction of time" suggests that it does not matter when a case is brought before the court of morality. Deciding. how to act presupposes the same legal process as passing a verdict on an action, in the present or the past, and whether of my own or of someone else. Clearly, there are good reasons for that view, grounded in a need for lawlike impartiality—or, rather, in a close association between lawlikeness and judicial impartiality. My decision on what to do next may be seen as my own judgment on what should be done. My capacity to take a right decision may relate to my capacity to imagine myself in a position of impartial judgment. My regrets for what I have done may stem from my judgment on what I should have done.

Two overlapping distinctions can be seen: between my decision and the verdict of others, and between past and present. They overlap in the sense that my later verdict on my own actions is to some degree the judgment of someone else: a later me, with a later view. (Thus cutting across any philosophical distinction between internal and external reasons: the reasons appreciated by my later self may have provided no motivation for my earlier self.[30]) Also, in deciding what to do next, I may give weight to how I and others will judge my action in the future. Both distinctions are relevant, but the latter one—between past and present—is linked more directly to the subject of this chapter. A timelessness in the moral law might not altogether exclude moral evolution, although genuine moral revolution would surely be hampered by the endurance, if not permanence, of moral concepts. The remark quoted from John von Neumann—that "all of us by now have developed the necessary code of ethics"—could be stretched to mean that by 1954 scientists had come to measure their new situation more appropriately against an existing code of ethics, or against an existing set of ethical concepts. Hence, perhaps, the source for regret, where "I should do x now" is projected back to "I should have done x then," as a continuing framework of estimation is seen to apply.

There are a number of differences between a decision to act and a judgment on an action, at a particular time or later.

First, the self who makes a choice may feel a different person from the same self later. By far the best analyst of this phenomenon was Proust, who went to enormous lengths to describe how falling in and out of love, the experience of grief or loss, and the mere passage of time made people different, altering not only the quality of their sensations but the nature of the subject. Against this is the point argued first by Locke that *person* is a "forensic term." This personality, he wrote, "extends itself beyond present existence to what is past, only by consciousness,—whereby it becomes concerned and accountable; owns and imputes to itself past actions, just upon the same ground and for the same reason as it does the present."[31] As his critics noted, the appeal to "consciousness" here was circular—what if one does *not* feel the same person who made a promise many years ago?—but Locke's underlying thought was plain enough: without a notion of continuous agency—personality—it is not easy to ground a notion of accountability.

Second, a present choice may at least *feel* free, and may *feel* as though it is being based on some consideration of obligations, interests, and motives. It may be possible to believe that in a present choice, a sense of obligation will be given precedence over interests and motives. It may even be possible to believe that freedom, or autonomy, is maximized insofar as a choice is liberated from interests and self-directed motives. A judgment or verdict on a choice—later, by a person making a choice, or by someone else—may take interests and motives—roughly speaking, causes rather than reasons—into account in a wholly different way. When deciding what to do, it may be self-deceiving for me to say to myself that I have no choice because of my background or external circumstances. But after I have chosen, or acted, or from a different perspective, it may not be irrelevant for my background and external circumstances to be taken into account as appropriate mitigation. This temporal asymmetry comes out ironically from an example constructed by Kant to show quite the opposite. He wrote of a person who tells a malicious lie as a "voluntary action" (*ein willkürliche Handlung*). The sources of this person's "empirical character" were to be found in "a bad upbringing, bad company" and also in "the wickedness of a natural temper insensitive to shame . . . carelessness and thoughtlessness . . . one does not leave out of account the occasioning causes. In doing all this one proceeds as with any investigation in the series of determining causes for a given natural event." But then

> even if one believes the action to be determined by these causes, one nevertheless blames the agent, and not on account of his unhappy natural temper, not on account of the circumstances influencing him, not even on account of the life he has led previously; for one presupposes that it can be entirely set aside how that life was constituted, and that the series of conditions that transpired might not have been, but rather that this deed could be regarded as entirely unconditioned in regard to the previous state, as though with that act the agent had started a series of consequences entirely from himself. This blame is grounded on the law of reason.[32]

The malicious liar's liability to be judged depended on his capacity to have acted otherwise. At the time of lying, the liar should not have been able to say to himself "my bad upbringing is causing me to lie." Even from the point of view of his own ("subjective") experience, he had been able to discriminate between the causes of his desire to lie and the reasons why he should not lie. And he should have realized

that the reasons should have trumped the causes. Yet after the event—
or at the same time, simply from a different perspective—causes for
the lie could certainly be seen. These might be valid mitigation, though
not for as harsh a judge as Kant.

The relevant change is a matter of knowledge. Maybe the liar could
be blamed if he had reasoned: "I had a bad upbringing which made me
a liar; I know that I ought not to lie; but my bad upbringing outweighs
the obligation." But what if he had been unaware of the effects of his
upbringing until his lawyer drew it to his attention at his trial: "Obviously
you lied because of your warped upbringing . . . this will be your defense"?
An evident difference between a decision and a judgment may be that
a decision has to be based on the knowledge available, even allowing for
an obligation to inform oneself as far as possible about whatever factors
may be relevant. This can apply not just to external factors (are the
Germans building a bomb?) but to the hazy line between reason and
cause in motivation (vanity, curiosity, patriotism?).

Third, a decision to act differs from a judgment on an action in
terms of commitment or engagement. Adam Smith tried to distinguish between the self as agent and the self as spectator or judge:

> When I endeavor to examine my own conduct, when I en-
> deavor to pass sentence upon it, and either to approve or
> condemn it, it is evident that, in all such cases, I divide myself,
> as it were, into two persons; and that I, the examiner and
> judge, represent a different character from that other I, the
> person whose conduct is examined into and judged of. The
> first is the spectator, whose sentiments with regard to my own
> conduct I endeavor to enter into, by placing myself in his
> situation, and by considering how it would appear to me,
> when seen from that particular point of view. The second is
> the agent, the person whom I properly call myself, and of
> whose conduct, under the character of a spectator, I was
> endeavoring to form some opinion. The first is the judge; the
> second the person judged of. But that the judge should, in
> every respect, be the same with the person judged of, is as
> impossible, as that the cause should, in every respect, be the
> same with the effect.[33]

And one of the reasons why this is impossible is that from the inside,
as it were, phenomenologically, making a choice is hardly the same as

judging a choice that one is about to make. With a yes-or-no decision
(Pascal: *il faut parier*) it may be too late not to choose (*vous êtes
embarqué*). One alternative may indeed result in a later verdict, where
another may mean that no judgment at all is applied. If Oppenheimer
had decided not to work at Los Alamos, it is more likely that we
would not be thinking about him at all than that we would be weigh-
ing up a judgment on that decision. This can be seen as one of the
features of so-called moral luck. To be pressed to a point of decision
may just be a matter of the bad luck of being the person in that
situation. Alternatively, there could be a more significant distinction
between choice and judgment. A choice may be unavoidable, but the
need for any judgment on it may vary.

Fourth, the very absorption of moral choice into a framework of
quasilegal judgment (as seen plainly in the language in the quotation
from Adam Smith) could be misleading: a point that came up earlier
in this study. Kant's view seems to have been that a decision would
not be a moral one unless it were taken within a framework of moral
law (which would be universal, necessary, and timeless). But why
assume that a choice to act has to be compared to a judgment on a
choice? Maybe there are many precedents or analogies that seem relevant, to the extent that what should be done will seem evident. But
what if there are not? Why try so hard to wash the singularity out of
a choice? Suppose instead that it were characteristic of moral choices
that the laws or rules under which they were to be taken were not at
all clear. You might know what to do if you only knew *which* rule to
apply or, more generally, under which description your action might
fall (Truman is very unlikely to have entertained the question: should
I be a mass-murderer? Just possibly he might have entertained the
question: will I be judged to have been a mass-murderer?). It might
just as well be characteristic of moral dilemmas that they can *not* be
resolved by appeal to generality, law, or precedent.

Against all of this, the readiest objection is that a choice or
decision may indeed differ in various ways from a judgment or verdict,
but that a (subjective) choice *should* be as much like an (objective)
judgment as possible. Nagel writes that "morality is possible only for
beings capable of seeing themselves as one individual among others
more or less similar in general respects—capable, in other words, of
seeing themselves as others see them."[34] More concretely, too much
concentration on (specific) choice rather than (general) laws or rules
might leave one too shortsighted to notice a slippery slope heading
toward unprincipled amoralism.

But this is to overlook the importance of time and change. Kant believed that a truly moral decision—a choice reasoned in the light of the moral law—was, or should be, neutral to time ("reason . . . recognizes no distinction of time"). In one way, that seems right. What I should do today, other things being equal, I should also do tomorrow or next week. What I should do now, I should also have done last week. (Perhaps some requirement to do something today and *only* today would be more like a merely conditional regulation than a categorical moral obligation.) To Kant, the moral world was timeless: "no before or after applies,"[35] while the order of natural causes took place within time. As his critics were quick to point out, the result might be that an apparently unique crisis, in which a choice of actions is wholly perplexing, may not qualify as a matter of morality, whereas a question that can be answered by a mechanical, algorithmic application of one of the formulae of the categorical imperative may qualify as moral. That may seem an unfair caricature, but, in fact, the problem created by time is not at all easy to avoid. The whole difficulty in a specific decision may relate to when it is taken—to the amount of knowledge available (or, often crucially, not available). A choice or decision may be almost literally dated. It may be impossibly difficult one day and could be easy the next. A judgment on a decision, of course, may be taken later, or it may be taken when its timing is no longer relevant, when all the relevant facts seem to be at hand. The Kantian ambition of making a decision as timeless as possible may not merely be counterfactual but may be in direct contradiction to the reality of a problem. The whole picture may be upside-down. In the question "What shall I do now?" it may be the *now* that is crucial. Its generalization may simply miss the point of the question. Nor is this an exceptional situation in which the background of relevant knowledge may be in constant change, as it can be with research.

In less abstract terms, the comment quoted at the beginning of this chapter from Secretary of War, Henry L. Stimson contained a perceptive thought: "I think the bomb . . . constitutes merely a first step in a new control by man over the forces of nature too revolutionary and dangerous to fit into the old concepts." What seemed new in 1945 was that old concepts no longer seemed to apply. This could be more than a figure of speech. At the Trinity test, Brigadier General Thomas F. Farrell noted, "All seemed to feel that they had been present at the birth of a new age."[36] The explosion of knowledge and understanding that came with the atomic bomb had a more lasting and more radical effect than the bomb itself.

It might seem natural to protest that the underlying fabric of morality—concepts of *ought, could, should*—will not change. Anyone could ask, at any time: What should I do? But moving from a position of ignorance to knowledge—or from partial knowledge to fuller knowledge—is not at all like a movement from one place, or viewpoint, to another (as the metaphor of "position" and "movement" assumes). It is a change through time, with the irreversibility that that implies. You can forget, or become confused, but you still do not go back to where you were. Spatial metaphor tends to be endemic to relativism (of both moral and intellectual varieties) and is—of course—deeply implausible. Going from one time to another is not at all like getting a better view by climbing higher uphill. "What should I do?" is only deceptively linked to "What should have been done?," even in thinking about the same action, at one time and then later. "What should I do?" can never be neutral in terms of time. To suppose otherwise must be to miss the force of the question.

Oppenheimer was asked to make a decision on a job in 1942. We can ask now—we may judge—whether he made the right decision. In 1942, it was predictable that the atomic bomb, if it worked, would change the balance of power overwhelmingly. It was foreseeable that there could be no safe defense and no guarantee against proliferation—again, if the bomb worked, and worked in time to be seen to work. It was not only predictable but entirely calculable that the bomb would be immensely destructive, maybe to the extent that its merely military use would be fanciful. And yet despite all this, a severe verdict—Oppenheimer could have known, so he should have known and so he should have chosen differently—would be ill-founded. The uncertainties in what was actually known were too great.

This is not a plea of mitigation. That would lead back toward the vacuity of "if only he had known." The world of 1942 in which a decision had to be made would be changed itself by the decision taken, and by its consequences. That could be said of many decisions, but the scale of the change from 1942 to 1945 was dramatic. It is possible to insist on a continuity in moral concepts, though that has to seem like waving a flag over the ruins devastated by an undeniable revaluation of values. It might be possible to insist on an autonomy of values from facts, though the facts of Hiroshima and Nagasaki might tend to drain this of plausibility. Anyone could see that notions of security, aggression, and power would have to be reworked. Any appeal to the legitimation of values by tradition would seem pointless (what price chivalry?).

Not many decisions can be important enough to affect the future of the world in a literal way. The Manhattan Project offered one of the first clear examples. The significance of a decision in science, with large practical effects, is that the world in which a later judgment is sought may not be the same as the world in which the decision was made, and the decision itself may have caused the difference. How far that is specific to science does not really matter, although the practical irreversibility of the growth in knowledge must be relevant. This can be seen as an extension of the routine thought—pursued in the previous chapter—that the consequences of actions may be unpredictable. In many circumstances, it may be hard to predict consequences, but with the search for new knowledge it may be impossible almost in principle.

CHAPTER SEVEN

PURITY

In his farewell speech at Los Alamos on November 2, 1945, Oppenheimer said of the bomb: "It is not an idea—it is a development and a reality."[1] One of the reasons why he is interesting—and so one of the reasons for this book—is that his ability was practical, in making things happen. He is famous not for having thought of the atomic bomb or for discovering the central theories behind it, but for getting it from theory into production within three years.

Oppenheimer's directorship at Los Alamos was his first job outside a university or a research institute, and his selection for it was a remarkable feat of intuition on the part of Groves. There could have been few signs that he would have the capacity to lead a huge project, and there might have been many signs to the contrary (including, his critics believed, his political unsuitability). As Jeremy Bernstein put it bluntly:

> The choice of Oppenheimer as the director of the Los Alamos Laboratory in 1942 struck most of his colleagues as almost incomprehensible. In the first place Oppenheimer was not a nuclear physicist. He was not even an experimental physicist; his early attempts to carry out experiments had been disastrous. He was not an engineer and had never run a large engineering project. He was notorious for getting arithmetic factors wrong. To add to all of this, he carried a burden of left-wing associations. His brother had been a member of the Communist Party and his wife had been married to a Communist. Some of his students had flirtations with the Party, and Oppenheimer himself—while certainly never a member

of the Party—had associations with organizations that had Communist front associations. It is unlikely that he could have been cleared to work on radar, which in the beginning of the war was the most important super-secret military project. Nonetheless, General Leslie Groves, who was in charge of the nuclear weapons program, chose him.[2]

Despite the rows and tantrums that might have been expected in such a hothouse, the general verdict is that the work was well led. Above all, it achieved its aims. By July 1945, Truman was able to meet Stalin at Potsdam in the knowledge that the United States had a working atomic bomb. The bomb was in use before the end of the war.

Oppenheimer tended to play down his purely scientific role. At one extreme, there is the view that the building of the bomb was a merely technical challenge—that after Meitner and Hahn's fission experiments of 1938–1939, or (more drastically) after the enunciation of the mass-energy equivalence by Einstein, the rest was just engineering. This view does not need to be taken seriously. It hardly seems likely that many of the best scientists in the world could have been challenged nonstop for two years by merely technical problems.

More significant now than any academic distinction between pure and applied science (or pure theory and applied technology) is the contrast between science, either pure or applied, and its realization; or between knowledge and practice. Among physicists in the early 1940s, it was very widely known that an atomic bomb might be possible. It was not difficult to see in outline how a bomb might be made. But the details were not trivial and their execution was not mere routine.[3] Heisenberg failed badly, though he knew the theory as well as anyone.

Reports of Oppenheimer at Los Alamos are unanimous: he knew everything and everyone. Weisskopf wrote, typically, in an obituary tribute:

> . . . his uncanny speed in grasping the main points of any subject was a decisive factor; he could acquaint himself with the essential details of every part of the work.
>
> He did not direct from the head office. He was intellectually and even physically present at each significant step; he was present in the laboratory or the seminar room when a new effect was measured, when a new idea was conceived. It

was not that he contributed so many ideas or suggestions; he did so sometimes, but his main influence came from his continuous and intense presence, which produced a sense of direct participation in all of us. It created that unique atmosphere of enthusiasm and challenge that pervaded the place throughout its time.[4]

Oppenheimer himself was more reserved: "it needs to be stated that many others contributed the decisive ideas and carried out the work which led to this success and that my role was that of understanding, encouraging, suggesting and deciding. It was the very opposite of a one-man show."[5]

❧

Book VI of Aristotle's *Ethics* contains the classic elaboration of the differences between theoretical knowledge (*epistêmê*), skill (*technê*), practical wisdom (*phronêsis*), and contemplative wisdom (*sophia*). Aristotle regarded practical wisdom as an intellectual virtue or excellence.[6] In contrast, Oppenheimer maintained a Platonic preference for science as knowledge against what he saw as technological capacity and political know-how. This can be seen in his harsh words quoted in chapter 5, about the "corrupt intrusion of scientists into other realms of which they have neither experience nor knowledge, nor the patience to obtain it."[7] (That was from 1948. By 1954 its irony would be painful. He must have been conscious that he had intruded far into the realm of the practical.) Paradoxically, at the end of the Manhattan Project he chose to stress that

> It is not possible to be a scientist unless you believe that the knowledge of the world, and the power which this gives, is a thing which is of intrinsic value to humanity, and that you are using it to help in the spread of knowledge, and are willing to take the consequences.[8]

In his later years, he had a good deal to say about the value and purity of science; for example, in his Reith Lectures of 1953, somewhat archly: "For most of us, in most of those moments when we were most free of corruption, it has been the beauty of the world of nature and the strange and compelling harmony of its order, that has sustained, inspirited, and led us. That also is as it should be."[9] In comparison, there was nothing about his immersion in practice.

Some may see this leaning toward pure knowledge as evasion. Jonathan Glover, for example, was unforgiving:

> Another attempted way of escape from moral responsibility is sometimes taken by those engaged in scientific research. This is to separate sharply "pure" research from the uses made of the knowledge it brings, in such a way that the former is uncontaminated by moral criticism of the latter.[10]

Oppenheimer's jarring references to "corruption" suggest that he would have felt the bite in this, though it would surely be fairer to take his words at face value—that he did esteem scientific knowledge in itself and that he held a comparatively lowly view of its technical realization. And yet the obvious irony is that he had put aside direct engagement in research to take charge of a scientific and technical tour de force. As Philip Kitcher has put it, in a tone more detached than Glover's, "Flourishing the label of purity isn't automatic. The label has to be earned"; pure researchers are those "whose lack of interest in the practical can be justified." Heidegger's hints about the interdependence of technology and pure science may not have been adequately supported in general terms, but they would have had some bearing on the work at Los Alamos.[11]

Oppenheimer may have been justified in his caution toward the view that "the scientist should assume responsibility for the fruits of his work."[12] The equivalence of mass and energy and the fission of the atomic nucleus were both discoveries that turned out to cause harm, but Einstein and Hahn did not intend to do harm in making them. Yet that could hardly apply to his own achievement at Los Alamos. Whatever the motivation of the scientists—patriotism, curiosity, ambition, fear of Hitler—there could be no uncertainty that the outcome was to be an immensely harmful weapon. For practical reasons, the vast plant manufacturing the materials for the bomb was a long way from Los Alamos; but a corresponding separation of practice from theory would have been meaningless. Any appearance of an ivory tower would be mistaken. As the technical history of the project says:

> However "pure" the scientists wanted their work to be, they were forced by the wartime circumstances to embrace the

methodology of Edison. That is to say, their objectives shifted from understanding to use, and from general conceptions to particular materials and apparatuses. This reorientation encouraged them to diversify their methodological toolkits with approaches typically employed by engineers and craftsmen, whose technical problems were anchored in concrete phenomena.[13]

Some questions about collective action and responsibility were raised in chapter 5. For now, the interest lies rather in the translation of theory into production. Platonic talk of pure knowledge that may only be contaminated by practice certainly misses the essence of Oppenheimer's achievement. An Aristotelian concentration on practical wisdom could miss the necessary dependence on physical theory. Glover's criticism is that responsibility may evaporate somewhere along a slippery slope from clean theory downhill to grimy practice. You cannot pin anything on Einstein for stating the mass-energy equation: he was engaged in the most abstract speculation. Nor just on the crew of the *Enola Gay* who dropped the bomb: they were obeying orders at the end of a long chain of command. You can point to the Commander in Chief; but then you may need to weigh up the difference between the office and the man. Truman, after all, knew nothing about the bomb until a time when its use was becoming almost irresistible. Roosevelt made the decision that turned theory into reality. In ruminations whether someone, or everyone, or no one, or everyone to differing degrees, was responsible, what can be missed is the presumption of a scale between pure theory and practice. Oppenheimer matters because he shows how misguided that presumption can be. In one way he looks as though he represents a perfect blend of nuclear physics with administrative, personal, and political know-how: the midpoint on a scale between theory and practice in terms of the development of the project, and thus in terms of responsibility. He came on to the scene when others had devised the theory and when others had decided to go ahead, when it was his job to make it work.

But in another way he shows how that perspective may be misleading. As seen in chapter 3, Oppenheimer himself was drawn to a conventionally sharp separation between advice and decision-making. For the scientist "it is good to turn over to mankind at large the greatest possible power to control the world and to deal with it according to its lights and values," and so on.[14] His experience in the late 1940s, and more severely in the early 1950s, was in government committees in charge of the development of nuclear weapons and nuclear power. Unsurprisingly, he came to hold a cautious view of the relations between politicians and scientists. But, from the start, the reality of his work did not fit into any point on a spectrum between scientific research and political control.

The work at Los Alamos was driven along the narrowest of paths to the tightest of deadlines by someone who understood every detail. That can be seen only in the loosest way as a translation of theory into practice, as though it was obvious what needed to be done and all that was needed was to will it into reality. Gerald Holton wrote that "the interlacing of the theoretical and experimental aspects was complete under Oppenheimer's influence and natural for all who worked with him."[15] As a model, *theory + plan + decision + will + resources = action* may seem naturally compelling, but that dissection fails to display the unity that was characteristic in Oppenheimer's work. No identifiable location is left for responsibility, allowing it to drain away or to be dispersed. We may or may not have some convincing account of action by an individual (on the one hand), and of collective action (on the other);[16] but (in between) we lack an account of how an individual can get a group to work together, and of what that implies for responsibility. In one way, Oppenheimer made the first atomic weapons as much as if he had assembled them with his own hands. But not, of course, alone. After Hiroshima, the White House claimed that what was new was "the achievement of scientific brains in putting together infinitely complex pieces of knowledge held by many men in different fields of science into a workable plan."[17] In the worlds of academic or scientific research, any disparagement of "administration," leadership, or "management" could be a symptom of unease with necessary organization. It might stem from some liberal optimism that projects can organize themselves freely, without direction. Further behind that could lie an uncertainty about how organization is to be understood. Responsibility or causality may be ascribed easily to an individual or, corporately, to a group. The rules of an association may include an allocation of responsibility in some legal sense ("the buck stops here"), but may give no clue as to how results may actually be achieved.

From the late nineteenth century onward, much thought was given to the place of intellectuals in society, presumably in the light of a worry that they might be superfluous in contrast with dynamic political activists (the word *intelligentsia* comes from early revolutionary Russia).[18] In comparison, less theoretical attention has been paid to the more substantial place of those who made direct impacts on events by putting new thought into practice. One striking exception, who has been studied in great detail, was Keynes, who combined the roles of first-rate economic innovator, polemical publicist, and, more significantly, economic-political strategist and negotiator. He was unusual, not just because of his huge talents, but because he operated in effect as a sole agent. He had many colleagues and supporters, but in his most influential period was hardly a real member of any organization. His preference to "remain footloose in the Treasury" during the Second World War, as his biographer puts it, was partly to allow himself more ease of maneuver, although it was also a sign of his own suspicion for a disengagement between theory and practice (as seen in his famous scorn for "practical men, who believe themselves to be quite exempt from any intellectual influences" but who in reality are "usually the slaves of some defunct economist").[19] The contribution of Oppenheimer, though, was definitely not as a solo operator, but as leader of a team. What he achieved was through the understanding, encouragement, and guidance of others. Clearly, this went beyond a narrowly legalistic or nominal sense of issuing orders for which he bore the responsibility. That type of achievement may now be less unusual than the kind of freelance individualism shown by Keynes, and far more elusive. The expansion of corporate power, government, and industrialized science may have reduced the scope for a single person to bring about identifiable change. As the steps from innovation to realization get more complicated and expensive, questions about how and whether to proceed with a project must become as common as questions about theoretical possibility. Certainly, it must become more likely that problems of choice or commitment will be met by individuals who work in organizations rather than as sole agents. Teller's bravado from 1947—that the development of pure and applied science "cannot and must not be stopped"[20]—has to be taken skeptically. Maybe—as discussed in chapter 4—the curiosity that leads to the development of pure science cannot be "stopped," and so the question whether it should or "must" be stopped may not arise. But the implementation of scientific discoveries undoubtedly *can* be stopped; and this is a point at which the philosopher's interrogation of the relationship between an *ought* and a *can* may be pressed, with good reason.

More immediately relevant now, the image of a scale or spectrum between polarities of pure theory and applied practice reflects an imagery of thought and action. An oversimple point might be that a clear dualism of mind and body feeds a dichotomy between plan and implementation, or theory and practice. On the one side, no blame can be attached to thinking: maybe original thought is spontaneous, involuntary, or unchosen. On the other, blame may attach to action. On a political level, a startlingly primitive faculty-psychology may be glimpsed behind a schism between advice and decision. Innovation, calculation, and the presentation of alternatives on the one side may be kept apart from decision-making and the willing of actions on the other. The point of this separation is that responsibility can be clearly pinned on decision-making, just as it is distanced from the tendering of advice: the bureaucrat's dream.

The analogy between faculties of the mind and organs of the state is Platonic: it runs right through the *Republic*.[21] There, those who took decisions would not be advised by experts with specialized knowledge. Knowledge itself would be a qualification for power. But there was still a clear separation between decision and execution. In the state it was evinced by the political-educational distinction between the guardian elite, qualified with knowledge, and the administrative class, equipped only with *technê*. It reflected a distinction between the deliberative and practical powers within the psyche. That can be still be seen now, even where there is a suggestion that distinct roles have been inverted as much as merged. Habermas notes:

> The dependence of the professional on the politician appears to have reversed itself. The latter becomes the mere agent of a scientific intelligentsia, which, in concrete circumstances, elaborates the objective implications and requirements of available techniques and resources as well as of optimal strategies and rules of control.[22]

This model might have its uses, but it has only a doubtful bearing on real politics. The decision to use the first atomic bombs rested with the office of the presidency—with Truman, who acted with copious military, diplomatic, and scientific advice. Constitutionally, of course, the president could have stopped everything at any stage. In practice, how far Truman could have put a brake on the Manhattan Project after he first heard about it in April 1945 could be an interesting question for historians.

This book is about different, less distinct decisions: not to use the bomb but to take part in building it and assume charge of building it. A political distinction between advice and decision could hardly be reflected within one individual. There, an internal theater of a consideration of options followed by an act of will could be only the most flimsy metaphor. In *Gemeinschaft und Gesellschaft*, Ferdinand Tönnies compared the natural, essential will (*Wesenwille*) to the arbitrary, calculative, rational will (*Kürwille*), "in the same way as the organic structure and individual organs of an animal body may be compared to a piece of apparatus or a *purpose-built* machine":

> natural will is rooted in the past and must be explained in its terms, as must things that are in the process of currently evolving; whereas rational, calculative, arbitrary will can be understood only with reference to developments in the future, by which it is brought to fruition. Natural will contains the future in embryo, while rational will contains it as an abstract image or hypothetical idea.

These dichotomies may be unsustainable as they stand, but they suggest a valuable insight. For Tönnies, the rational will was intrinsically estranging or alienating, even "within the human subject."[23] In his terms, that would have been true almost by definition in that he saw rational calculation, somewhat romantically, as external to natural human ends. (This must have owed something to a Marxian notion of alienation). Less ambitiously, the larger the step from theory to practice, or from planning to execution, the more abstract or depersonalized one might expect decision-making to be. At a political or institutional level that would scarcely be surprising. Here, we would be in the realm of *Gesellschaft*, not *Gemeinschaft*: decision by calculation in an administrative bureaucracy, not by the immediate will of a ruler or of a *Volk*.

More relevantly, any assumed distinction between private, "mental" decision-taking and public, overt action is itself one that needs examination. An underlying presumption, again, might be that reflection—theory—may be spontaneous and free, whereas implementation—application—might be subject to social constraint. Certainly, it is not hard to run together arguments for free inquiry with arguments on behalf of rights to privacy. With both there might be a desire to define a sphere for the individual's thinking, beyond any scope for external interference. Such efforts have been subject to much discussion and criticism.[24] But whatever the origins or defects of any distinction between private thought and public action, the applicability of that distinction must surely be questionable here. In terms of the discussion in chapter 3, on curiosity, it might just be plausible to say that private thought—theoretical research—has to be beyond constraint, if only because of the practical limits to any imaginable form of control.[25] Again, following the discussion in chapter 4, there could be a good case that a blanket of responsibility should not extend over those whose thought led to consequences that could never have been foreseen. (Why stop with Einstein? Why not blame Newton or Galileo?) The trouble is that none of these distinctions or dichotomies are directly helpful with the real problem in this chapter. Oppenheimer's work at Los Alamos was in no sense either pure research or mere implementation, either pure thought or mere action. Teller's *Memoirs* at least provide a useful reminder of that:

> The newly established laboratory procedures were as strange as our setting. Almost all of us were accustomed to an academic atmosphere, to having time to sit and think quietly by ourselves. . . . But at Los Alamos, almost constant collaboration was necessary, all the work was done at a feverish pace, and one's new good idea, once hatched, could be taken away and given to others to develop. . . .
>
> In addition, theoretical physicists, unused to considering the practical, had to involve themselves in engineering problems. Everything about the project was novel. While one group of scientists worked to develop a supporting theory, other scientists struggled with the practical details for the execution on the basis of the current best guess in the hope of completing the project at the earliest possible time.[26]

Insofar as any question of scientific ethics could be located here, it could hardly be as simple as whether to think some new thought. With the Manhattan Project, the steps from theoretical conception to practical implementation were so elaborate and expensive that remorse for the initial discovery would have been almost beside the point.

The central problem is no less real because it is hard to clarify. *Making something happen* should be unambiguous enough. What Oppenheimer did was not limited to the fact that he acted as the appointed head of the project. There need be nothing misleading in placing him in a sui generis role. Jeremy Bernstein has taken the view that "during the war he became one of the greatest laboratory directors who ever lived"; although that can lead back to questions about the character of the greatness and to the indeterminacy of a point on any scale between initially pure research and subsequently applied implementation. Even more strongly—Bernstein again—"the bomb would probably not have been built by the summer of 1945 were it not for Oppenheimer."[27] The identification of Oppenheimer as a necessary condition for the project goes beyond the idea of just a driving force, to the point where it could be seen as his project. Groves, at least, seems to have realized that what Oppenheimer could offer was not available elsewhere, and the confidence that he was irreplaceable continued throughout the war despite a ceaseless grumble of suspicion from Groves's security advisors.

Here is a recollection of the notion of the authorship of action mentioned in chapter 2. In that *what Oppenheimer did* was his own achievement, not easily imagined to be achieved by another, there should be no surprise that it seems hard to categorize. If one part of the bureaucrat's dream is a dissociation between advice and decision-making, another is surely an ideal of impersonal action—here we are back with Tönnies—where what is done is done not by a person but by an officeholder: where the bureaucrat who drops dead at his desk can be succeeded without difficulty by another who picks up his pen and carries on writing. That caricature is at the polar opposite from any notion of individual authorship or achievement, where what can be passed on, or taken over by another, is exactly what does not matter. One simple measure of an achievement is how hard it would be for anyone else to have performed the same task, or to have taken it over before completion.

This must be a point of interest for the moral philosopher or for anyone thinking about evaluation. An action or activity that is hard to specify is also hard to evaluate. There are obvious temptations to seize on points where evaluation can be applied easily: intentions to act, weighable outcomes, actions that can be appraised regardless of who performs them. One attraction of generalization or universalizability is that is does promise straightforward pegs on which to hang evaluations: this act, if done by anyone. . . . Richard Hare: "If I

call a thing a good X, I am committed to calling any X like it good."[28]
Perhaps so, but what if there is nothing much like X or we are not
sure what X is?

A shortcoming in an antithesis between pure and applied knowledge is that any location for personal evaluation can get lost between
the two. It should not matter who unearths an item of pure knowledge. Part of the Platonic ideology of pure knowledge is that it is *there*
to be discovered, making the discoverer secondary to the discovery. *It
could have been anyone* can be true beyond professional modesty. With
applied knowledge, *it could have been anyone* has a different sense,
where rightness or wrongness may attach as much to an action as to
the agent. But that could be misleading in more than one way. In an
important sense actions can *belong* to someone. On the whole, a court
of law does not determine whether certain actions are illegal, but
whether individuals have committed illegal actions.

This is far more than a theoretical quibble. There can be genuine uncertainty about where to attach judgment, responsibility, or
blame to practical decisions made by a scientist. Oppenheimer may
have been attracted by a mirage of purity, where individual responsibility might have no bearing. But, equally, he knew that the work at
Los Alamos was not pure research. Perhaps there ought to be some
contrast between the work at Los Alamos and his decision to contribute to it. Yet that contrast loses its point if the work would not have
succeeded as it did without his contribution. (There is some analogy
with the work of Heisenberg in Germany. We cannot know how
essential he was to it, in a sense in which alternatives may have
existed, but we can know that whatever was or was not achieved was
inseparable from his contribution.) Goaded by a stream of foolish and
malevolent questions in the 1954 hearing, Oppenheimer remarked: "I
think I need to point out that to run a laboratory is one thing. To
advise the government is another."[29] The distinction he may have
had in mind was not so much between political action and bureaucratic or scientific advice as between what he had been doing before
and after 1945. His choice in 1945 was to continue as an advisor in
an area where he had become a leading expert among many others.
His choice in 1942 had been to take a job for which it happened he
was the only candidate.

Any hesitation or uncertainty we feel may be the legacy of limitations in an older way of assigning praise and blame. Old moral and
legal traditions knew how to deal with the hand that holds the knife

or the king who utters the command. Now, courts of law may appor-
tion responsibility within an organization, normally in some hierarchical order, but it must be doubtful whether any moral instinct or
reaction could be so finely graduated. There can be older feelings
about proximity to harm that may be as undeniable as they are indefensible. Perhaps we should be as shocked by someone who inciner-
ates a town from the air as by someone who dispatches a town full of
people individually by hand, face-to-face; the reality, regrettably or
not, is different. Equally, monstrous wrongs may pollute indiscrimi-
nately, regardless of narrowly appraised responsibility. There could be
an historical argument that a lack of focus in choice or responsibility
is a result of a shortcoming in our moral concepts, which have not
kept up with the times. So maybe we need some conceptual analysis,
development, or improvement?

If moral concepts grew spontaneously, as offshoots of practical
changes, then surely the right approach would be either to await
appropriate conceptual growth or to accept that whatever conceptual
apparatus we have now must already be appropriate to our situation.
A converse view would be that any understanding of actions—of
what people do, and have done—must depend on the concepts through
which they are identified (or the language by which they are described). Such concepts must contain some moral import, even if a
supposedly neutral one (as when a neutral massacre or murder might
be called a killing). Plainly, neither perspective can be entirely right
or wrong. On the one hand, no one needed to think about the ethics
of nuclear warfare in the eighteenth century. On the other, it would be
hard to argue that any notion of responsibility or agency could be
independent of some background of moral concepts. Facts may help to
form morality, but morality also shapes facts. By 1954, John von
Neumann, as quoted in the last chapter, sounded confident that "all of
us by now have developed the necessary code of ethics."[30] Obviously,
such development was partly in response to the invention of atomic
weaponry, but that response must have included an adjustment of existing feelings, thoughts, and prejudices to a new predicament.

At some basic level, as Elizabeth Anscombe put it, "there are
many descriptions of happenings which are directly dependent on our
possessing the *form* of description of intentional actions."[31] The
difficulties we face in thinking about the application of pure science,
or the role of the pure scientist who becomes entangled in practical
application, could be a reflection of a shortcoming in the language of

moral description and hence moral discrimination. In the most evident sense, Oppenheimer did not know what he was going to *do* when he agreed to take charge in 1942. He was going to *lead* a project that would *try to build* a bomb. What he *did* then could be put in wildly different ways: *advancing* nuclear physics, *helping to save* Europe from Hitler, *preparing* the destruction of Hiroshima and Nagasaki, *ending* the Second World War, *striking the first blow* of the Cold War. What he chose to do in 1942 was not the same as what he ended up doing: the task developed, the possible descriptions proliferated. This must be commonplace, especially in wartime. Oppenheimer's own preference was for a narrowly restricted description. In his words, his role "was that of understanding, encouraging, suggesting and deciding"(and not "policy-making").[32] This must have been in deliberate, deflating contrast to the more grandiose descriptions of contemporary popular legend: Father of the Bomb, and so on. More significantly now, it was also in contrast to the uninformative terms that are all we have: leading, directing, guiding, managing. If morality shapes facts, here the language of description lags far behind practice.

The thinness of the available language must be significant, and may induce a temptation to reach impatiently for reductive common sense or for law: Oppenheimer was a necessary condition for the Manhattan Project. Without him, it would not have worked as it did. Whether or not that is correct, no one could have known it in advance, in 1942. What he was asked to do, and what he decided on doing, was not to be indispensable but to recruit, plan, organize, calculate, and build. His choice in 1942 was to take charge of work on weapons that might turn out to have enormous destructive power. Whatever his motives, he and many others believed sincerely and with good reason that in Germany Heisenberg might be engaged in a parallel project. Whether that is an excuse or exculpation, it does provide one clear, minimal account of what Oppenheimer believed he was choosing to do at the start: to keep ahead of a German atomic bomb project.

Once more, the contrast with Heisenberg can be illuminating. There can be factual debate over what Heisenberg actually did after 1939—in pedantic terms, under which concepts his actions or inaction are to be described—he made a mistake, dragged his feet (consciously or not), did his best, supported the Führer, worked for his country, became carried away by scientific curiosity, aimed to frustrate atomic research, and so on. He and his collaborators never believed—

even at the end of the war—that the Americans and the British were capable of building an atomic bomb; as shown by his astonishment on hearing the news of Hiroshima.[32] Enough was known of Hitler for anyone to realize that he was not the man to be in control of an overwhelmingly powerful weapon. It is hard to imagine any defense for what Heisenberg even started to do, partly because he—or anyone—could have known in 1939 that the only imaginable outcomes from a successful German atom bomb project would be bad. What Heisenberg knew in 1939, when he chose to return from the United States to work in Germany, and what Oppenheimer knew in 1942, when he chose to take charge of the atomic bomb project, were wholly different.

None of this, of course, gets us far with what Oppenheimer did after 1942, and what he chose to do after 1944, when the threat of a German bomb became unlikely, and then nonexistent. His withdrawal from the project might have made a serious difference. If he had joined his many colleagues who expressed qualms about the use of the bomb in the spring of 1945, its use on Hiroshima and Nagasaki might have become less inexorable. But these can only be speculations. Traditional views of responsibility make little allowance for the momentum in a large project, as though a decision to join at the start were indistinguishable from a decision to stay on board every day thereafter. This is not new. Any of the individuals in a medieval cavalry charge would have been free to stop and turn back, just as any scientist at Los Alamos could have left without too much difficulty, as did Joseph Rotblat in 1944.[34]

❧

Again, there is a need to distinguish between looking at Oppenheimer and looking at ourselves looking at Oppenheimer. There are at least two areas where we should look first at the competence of our own judgments, and the means by which they are reached: how to assess a contribution to practical management or organization in a large, complicated, scientific-technical project; and how to appraise a contribution where it is exactly its unique character that creates much of the interest. In both areas, as elsewhere, an emphasis upon individual responsibility, in the sense of necessary-condition causality, has distinct drawbacks, whatever its traditional cultural power. In both areas, an implicit resort to a legal model of judgment is either unhelpful or misleading. There can be some distance between a simple (but ill-defined) notion of who did what and a simple (but clear) notion of moral or legal answerability. *What Oppenheimer did* can slide uneasily up and down a gradient from pure science to practical administration. In some straightforward sense, what he did is plain enough. Yet the disparities in descriptions remain striking, as shown in the two quotations near the beginning of this chapter, for example, between his own "understanding, encouraging, suggesting and deciding" and Weisskopf's remark that he was "intellectually and even physically present at each significant step." The uniqueness of Oppenheimer's contribution causes strains in another way. Any attempt to characterize an action *like that*—where he could be appraised against some presumed measure of how another person might have acted, or how he might have acted himself if circumstances had been altered—seems to extinguish the reasons why his predicament is of interest in the first place. Attempts to pronounce on The Role of the Scientist just miss what made Oppenheimer's role important when it was. Yet, obviously, if there are no wider conclusions to be drawn, there could not be much point in looking at his life: hence the tension between philosophy and biography aired in chapter 1.

What this chapter should reveal is the frailty of the apparatus with which we identify and appraise some important questions. An orthodox response would be to suggest some broadening of a concept of individual, personal answerability. Our view—our problem—it might be thought—derives from our need to reach a judgment, combined with an aversion to collective responsibility. In the background lies a legalistic model of the individual on trial. There are entirely understandable historical reasons for all this; but—so it might be thought—one consequence is that no verdict can be returned when the role of an individual cannot be securely pinned down and the context of judgment offers no guidance by way of precedent or comparison. So if we want to retain a desire to judge, we may need to shift our framework of appraisal away from the contribution of the individual and toward something more collective. That has been a temptation in thinking about war crimes, genocide, and the legacies of colonialism and slavery.[35] But there are two serious difficulties. Morally, collective indictment seems a questionable weapon to borrow from those who may have been too ready to wield it themselves. Worse, there must be doubt about how far "we" are in any position to advocate changes from allegedly individualist to collectivist perspectives. This could be because of the ineffectiveness of winding back the clock to what can be seen as a more primitive view. (Judgments that "we" are all guilty of some past collective crime may do little more than make us uncomfortable.) Less speculatively, "our" concepts of choice, freedom, agency, causality, responsibility, and blame are so intimately tied to a concept of action by an individual that maybe they just cannot be stretched without damage to cover anything else.

More radically, such a net of conceptual connections could be entangled with the very idea of judgment: "our" wish for judgment. Not necessarily in a sense of condemnation—bluntly, where there is a need to find someone to blame—but in terms of understanding. One problem explored in this chapter has been how to understand the kind of contribution made by Oppenheimer. It must be significant that the clearest possible framework of understanding—for identifying an individual location between theory and practice—is legal. Particularly in military law there is an elaborate scheme of rules and precedents to establish legitimate authority to issue orders, when they must and may not be obeyed, who takes responsibility, and when all rules may be overridden. The need for a verdict creates a context in which a judgment can be reached and through which an individual's actions can be understood. But can this model apply when no context of judgment exists: not merely no legal rules and precedents but no unequivocal requirement for a decision? There may be cases where an action is understood in terms of a known—legalistic—context. (The framework for understanding the varieties of causing death, most clearly, derives much of its import from law. *Murder* hardly has an inexact sense, and its exact sense comes from extensive legal definition.) But does it follow either that if a determining context is lacking, understanding becomes problematic, or that where there is a failure to understand it must be because some such context of judgment is lacking? If we understand through judging, what if we try not to judge?

Here, the point would be that our desire to judge—to reach a verdict—is tied to a notion of individual responsibility that is hard to reconcile with the nature of Oppenheimer's achievement. The difficulty in fixing a settled description of what he did—for example, its location between pure and applied science—derives from our wish to make a judgment on the past; we have no framework for judgment other than one of legally modeled individual accountability. The description we seek tends to swerve between building, directing, deciding, encouraging, and so on. A simple response might be that of course we have trouble in characterizing the kind of contribution made by Oppenheimer because it was so new—he was the first leader of a huge military–scientific–industrial project—and it need not be surprising that past concepts fail to cover it. Maybe future conceptual—or legal—developments will remedy this shortcoming. But, again, the issue must be more challenging than that. Uncontroversially, language and frameworks of law may evolve in line with moral or social feelings. Then what about those feelings?

The trouble is that a clear focus does not help. We want to ask what Oppenheimer did: or, in general terms, what was the nature of his role as research director, project manager, or whatever? It was plainly not "pure" research, however that is understood. It was not mere implementation of pure research by others. Any understanding of his contribution will imply some judgment. What he knew about the possibility of a German atomic bomb, for example—a straightforwardly factual question—is hardly neutral in its implications for how his actions are understood. Some possible descriptions, or judgments, are surely excluded. How far are the terms through which actions are interpreted or understood formed by terms of individual responsibility or blame? Any attempt to understand fully will imply some verdict on moral responsibility. To understand must be to articulate. To articulate must be in part to judge. To judge is to appraise individual responsibility.

A general point would be that our wish to judge the past, either in an everyday sense or as moral philosophers, could be an unavoidable legacy of a God's-eye perspective. We want a context or perspective for description or understanding that enables us to reach a verdict, but the only one at hand will not work. The terms we have cannot be neutralized easily. *Judge not, that ye be not judged* had an evident theological context. It may still provoke moral philosophers who no longer accept that context to ask from where, and on what basis, judgments can be made.

CHAPTER EIGHT

THE LESSONS OF HISTORY

Kant produced this prospectus for his classes on ethics in 1765–1766:

> Ethics. Moral philosophy has this special fate: that it takes on
> the semblance of being a science and enjoys some reputation
> for being thoroughly grounded, and does so with even greater
> ease than metaphysics, and that in spite of the fact that it is
> neither a science nor thoroughly grounded. The reason why
> it presents this appearance and enjoys this reputation is as
> follows. The distinction between good and evil in actions, and
> the judgment of moral rightness, can be known, easily and
> accurately, by the human heart through what is called senti-
> ment, and that without the elaborate necessity of proofs. In
> ethics, a question is often settled in advance of any reasons
> which have been adduced—and that is something which does
> not happen in metaphysics. It will not, therefore, come as a
> surprise that no one raises any special difficulties about admit-
> ting grounds, which only have some semblance of validity. For
> this reason, there is nothing more common than the title of a
> moral philosopher, and nothing more rare than the entitlement
> to such a name.[1]

In his later, far more famous, writings he sought to adduce "reasons"
that would not only allow for the "distinction between good and evil
in actions, and the judgment of moral rightness" but would also serve
to characterize or define the nature of morality. This early text is
interesting in showing an order of thought that did not change in his
later work. First, we do know about good and evil and moral rightness.

135

Then we seek to adduce reasons. At least, that was the thinking castigated by Nietzsche in the sections on the "Natural History of Morality" in *Beyond Good and Evil*: philosophers—Kant was mentioned shortly afterward—believed they could provide a "ground" (*Begründung*) for morality, but they took their morality for granted, as "given."[2] More generally, in his notebooks, Nietzsche made an opposition between what he called "two different kinds of philosophers": "those who have to hold fast some large body of valuations, that is of previous assignments and creations of value (logical or moral ones), and then those who are themselves the legislators of valuations."[3]

We need not be so ambitious in aiming to be "legislators," but we can agree that Nietzsche did identify a real problem, which is particularly evident from some of the discussions in this book. We—whoever "we" are—may well have opinions on the rightness of Oppenheimer's choice in 1942, and on the good or evil in his subsequent actions. We may seek "grounds" for our opinions. For example, we may think that Oppenheimer chose wrongly (or rightly) because (in principle) a scientist should not engage in research on weapons, except (on principle) where greater harm could be averted. Or we may think that he chose rightly because one outcome of his choice in 1942 was the ending of the war in August 1945, rather than later, with a greater loss of life. So our opinions may be grounded in—or supported by—principles or calculations, though the details of those principles and calculations might be contested to the point of delivering no clear verdict. In such ways morality, or moral principles and calculations, might be taken as "given." (Such is the assumption, for example, of Michael Walzer, of a "common morality" shared in the judgments "we" make.[4]) But in another way we may not know, or may be uncertain, about judgments that call for grounding, or whether there is a place for judgments at all. The problem is not a vindication of morality as much as its scope, function, and location. A primitive starting-point might well be—as Nietzsche would see it—some inclination to moralize, or pass judgments, about a choice, and a series of decisions and actions, where morality should surely have something to say. But whose morality, and where; and what about contradictory intuitions that any moral verdict would be wholly inappropriate, pointless, or out of place?

Some of these difficulties have come up already. Insofar as previous chapters may have seemed inconclusive, that may not be because established moral criteria deliver inconclusive results. Rather the opposite. There could be a clear enough calculation that the net consequences of the Hiroshima and Nagasaki bombs might come out as positive, not negative. There could be a case in favor of Oppenheimer's duty to join and lead the Manhattan Project. Any uncertainty lies in finding such verdicts at all decisive, or in defending them against possible objections. And only part of such uncertainty stems from the thoughts about a new moral world aired in chapter 6. Things may have changed irreversibly at Alamogordo, but that kind of irreversible change was itself not unique. The problem it raised is common to any decision made in which the outcome radically alters the terms of the initial predicament in which the decision is presented. That need not be a matter of huge scale, as it was at Alamogordo. Medical developments can modify the questions asked about life or death, as well as offer changed answers. (And it is ironic that consequentialist ethics have such appeal for many with an interest in bioethics, given that the assessment of incalculable consequences would seem to create an unavoidable impediment.) A more basic issue discussed in chapter 6 does lead on to a more general problem, about the relation between a choice—or specifically a moral choice—and time. What Oppenheimer did was rooted essentially in when he did it, both in terms of his own life and in terms of the historical context. In one way that looks trivial. In another it calls for further thought. It will come up again later in this chapter. The other chapters in this book should lead to some similarly basic issues.

CHOICE

Chapter 2 was concerned with Oppenheimer's point of choice. The question of where judgment is to be applied is not a merely theoretical one. If we feel—and of course we may not—that Oppenheimer's actions were open to approval or disapproval, then some chain of reflection looks unavoidable: Which actions? Which choices? When? This book has concentrated on his decision to take on the work at Los Alamos, rather than even less clear decisions implied by his continuation in that work or by his participation in planning for the use of the bombs. But the focus we need is not improved by identifying some specific day toward the end of 1942 and asking whether he chose rightly or wrongly then. That is not the sort of clarity which is problematic. The model that eases, or simplifies, matters for us is one of an individual making an individual free choice at a particular time, leaving us to ask whether the choice was right or whether it should have been made differently. Our role then, if we want one, is in bestowing or in withholding approval. We might consider how far the model is suitable.

Oppenheimer's remark that "I do not think that the Nazis allow us the option"[5] (in going ahead with research on the bomb) obviously cannot have been meant as an abnegation of free will in a sense of denying his ability to act otherwise at any point. Whatever it meant, it was not a denial of his autonomy in choosing to act. It is sterile to press the question: could he have said no? (Sakharov could have said no when told to take his part in the construction of Soviet nuclear weapons, but then he might have been shot. How fruitful is it to debate that kind of freedom?) The earlier discussion brought up notions of acceptance and authorship, in contrast with a plainer notion of choice. Despite his embittered remark that "I would have done anything that I was asked to do,"[6] to say that Oppenheimer accepted the responsibility he was offered is not to suggest that he was passive, rather than choosing actively. It is to emphasize that the position for him in 1942 is not best seen as a selection between either–or alternatives.

Much depends on the model assumed. It could be legalistic: was he free to say no? Should he have acted as he did? Or it could be authorial, as it would be in: should he have written that book? Either way, the answer could be simply yes or no, but the difference lies in the separation between the agent and the act. In legal terms we may separate the action from the person who performs it. In authorial terms this cannot be sustained in the same way. We can of course look at texts without regard to the lives of their authors, either as a matter of critical policy or of necessity (with ancient inscriptions, for example). But it is surely pointless to imagine that a choice for me to produce a particular work can ever be the same as a choice for anyone else to produce it. Legal assessment may look like an easier model for what we believe to be moral appraisal. Guilt or innocence in court certainly seem like apt parallels for responsibility or nonresponsibility out of court. We know where we are with this. Yet there can also be critical judgments, as well as more straightforward judgments of authorship: did he really write (or do) this? Was it any good?

This is not to advocate a use of aesthetic standards in ethics: the history of "beautiful deeds" has been a catastrophic one. Rather, at the least, it is to point out how inadequately one way of looking at things helps us to see. The outcome should not be merely some kind of excuse or mitigation, as where what may have been right or wrong for Oppenheimer in 1942 cannot be appraised in the same way as what may have been right or wrong for anyone else at any other time. An understandable response then would be the argument used by Oppenheimer's lawyer, quoted in chapter 1: "Does this mean that you should apply different standards to him than you would to somebody like me or somebody else that is just ordinary? No, I say not. I say that there must not be favoritism in this business."[7] In a courtroom—which is effectively where this was—that may have been a prudent forensic line. But why behave as though we are in a courtroom? Why assume that our judgment has to be like a legal judgment? If we are reflecting on the nature of moral appraisal, to assume this may be to beg the question, in denying at the outset what may turn out to be the case, that a central feature of moral appraisal could be that it is not lawlike at all.

Again, precedent may be an important strand in legal thinking. In plain terms, an action *like that* has been seen as right or wrong in the past, compelling some similar view for the future. And we have seen in looking at Oppenheimer's point of choice how hard it could be to nail down a repeatable decision that could have been distilled from his position in 1942. A conventional response might be that here we meet the normal complexities of real life (and hence the conclusion that there can be no edifying lessons from history). A different response might be that the entire enterprise of reading from the past to the present or the future, where the whole idea of identifying a choice *like that*, was misguided from the outset.

The discussion in chapter 2 should have raised some doubts about where we think any kind of appraisal might be applied. Once more, maybe we want to look for a clear point of choice where we can see a yes-or-no decision that would have made all the difference, and where we can apply a judgment for or against. One does not need to be a determinist to suspect questions about past points of choice. In many cases, a judgment that someone should or should not have done something is unavoidable. Verdicts may be needed. But how far is this typical or exceptional? It may not be helpful for moral clarity to blur points of decision. It may have been valuable both to Caesar and his opponents to know that the Rubicon marked a clear point of no return. On the other hand, the same example can be used in the opposite way. The only sensible response to the question "What should Caesar have done at the Rubicon?" might be that he should not have arrived there with an army at all. Questions like "What should he have done?" have evident uses, but we must keep in mind how much they take for granted: in the case of Caesar (or Oppenheimer) that for him, as and where he was, he could have accepted some alternative. There, the traditional philosophical emphasis is on *could*. Instead, it might be on *for him* and as and where he was.

Further, why accept that we are in a position of judging at all? Because we may want to ask whether he was right to make a particular choice, and that looks like a question of judgment. This could be important in turning our attention away from Oppenheimer and toward ourselves and what we think we are doing, or toward the nature and function of what we may take to be moral appraisal. Many twentieth-century writers approached such questions by looking into what they believed to be the characteristic general features of moral judgments or the language used to embody them. But that takes the path criticized by Nietzsche, in assuming that we know what morality is and then asking what characterizes it. In somewhat different terms, "What should he have done?" implies some context of judgment. We may want to repudiate what Kant might have regarded as noncategorical contexts for the question ("What should he have done to: improve his career—quench a thirst for blood—win the war—forestall Nazi physics—&c?") in favor of a purely moral reading ("What *should* he have done?"). Which of course returns us to our assumptions about what we count as moral, and to the risk that a purified context may turn out to be a purely empty one.

VALUE

The point for choices might seem to occur where the known facts run out, or when there is no agreement about ends or values. As seen in chapter 3, questions of value may be connected with questions of who is to choose and on the basis of what information, at least in matters of scientific and political choice. One idealized model is where knowable facts are assembled by scientific advisors and where choices of ends or values are taken by legitimate political decision-makers. The underlying alignment between facts-knowledge-reason-expertise-science on the one side and values-opinion-will-authority-politics on the other assumes a judgment on the place and priority of value or morality: it becomes what is left over when the facts are clear. Plainly, this does not represent a neutral standpoint on the nature of moral choice. With any of this in mind, debates about whether the facts of nuclear weaponry do or do not imply any particular judgments of value must be loaded at the outset. Value interpreted as the field of the will—or worse, of choice based on uncertainty—in contrast with fact as the field of reason and knowledge, starts with a residual sense and is destined to shrink.

Alternatively, against a background of agreed ends or values, choices may be seen as pure calculation. The invention and use of a bomb would have such-and-such outcomes agreed as beneficial and such-and-such agreed as not beneficial, and agreed criteria might be available to measure the balance without appeal to further judgments of value. If everything is agreed, then obviously there is no room for disagreement, moral or political. (This could be one version of decisions made between 1942 and 1945. One reason why there was strikingly little debate is that almost all those who knew about the Manhattan Project were agreed on its immediate aims.) The scope for choice can either be left to those not concerned with the pursuit of facts or it can be reduced to value-free accountancy (as in the games-theory calculations of the Rand Corporation's sages in the 1950s). Either way, any room for discussion of connections between fact and value is restricted by the diminished, secondary scope for value. Richard Evans, in his study of the aims and nature of history, brings this out explicitly. Moral judgment becomes "extraneous":

> ... there is surely a moral element involved in all kinds of research in the natural sciences, from embryology to nuclear physics. Moral concerns may drive scientific research, or they may emerge from it; the key point surely is that, just as in history, the element of moral judgment, insofar as it is exercised at all, is in the end extraneous to the research rather than being embedded in the theory or methodology of it.[8]

It might be equally unsatisfactory to reverse this priority, in the manner of Levinas, by trying to insist that value somehow precedes fact, instead of being an inexplicable residue. A more defensible view might be to point out how easily any demarcation between fact and value may be question-begging. The notion of a pure, value-free fact can only be isolated in contrast with some notion of value that itself may be characterized in residual contrast with facts. This appears most painfully with outrageous examples, such as an extermination camp—or an atomic bomb—where the strain in producing a value-free description must be evident. The point is not that we are somehow ("logically") unable to do this, but that what we assume in doing it is itself not value-free. This is borne out even by well-used examples that might seem to count against it. Hume asked his readers to "take any action allow'd to be vicious: Wilful murder, for instance. Examine it in all lights, and see if you can find that matter of fact, or real existence, which you call vice." His conclusion, naturally, was that "you can never find it, till you turn your reflection into your own breast." Yet he was not denying the existence of value; this was a fact itself: "Here is a matter of fact; but 'tis the object of feeling, not of reason." And his argument only worked at all (insofar as it did) on the assumption of the existence of "any action allow'd to be vicious." The presence of value was taken for granted by Hume at the outset.[9]

The first atomic bomb may be seen as a lump of metal: a morally neutral fact. The bomb might also be seen as the product of a huge act of will on the part of politicians, scientists, engineers, and soldiers, with a huge political, scientific, financial, and military value: a surfeit of values. Its origin was hardly irrelevant, as though it sprang into existence in 1945 leaving only a question of what to do with it. It was the outcome of innumerable decisions about means and ends. The idea of an absence of values looks like the opposite of the truth.

CURIOSITY

A paradox was created by Oppenheimer's thoughts on the value of inquiry—of curiosity—pursued in chapter 4 ("If you are a scientist you cannot stop such a thing. If you are a scientist you believe that it is good to find out how the world works"[10] and so on). The hope seemed to be that the pursuit of knowledge was a self-evident duty, to the extent that any disagreement would be seen in terms of impediment, control, or restraint. This hope was maintained together with a belief that facts were facts, and whatever was done with them was a matter of will or choice. In reality, the value of research is a textbook case of ideology, with obvious historical and cultural roots. Of course this is not to deny that the pursuit of knowledge has a value. It is only to recall that this value has easily identifiable origins. The appropriate response should not be to claim that the pursuit of knowledge has some other sort of value or no value at all. That would justify complaints that the value of research might be subordinated to some other supposed values, as where "humane" or religious priorities might be superimposed. Instead, there might be some relevance in Nietzsche's suggestion of links between value and what he called "an interpretation, a way of interpreting" (elsewhere he wrote of "familiar perspectives and valuations").[11] An alternative to "If you are a scientist, you believe that it is good to find out how the world works" might be not "If you are a scientist, you believe that it is not good to find out how the world works," but that you might believe something wholly different, whether a scientist or not. You might not start, for example, from an assumption of a value-free world of fact. The difference is not over what is to be valued but over where and how value applies at all. "Scientific ethics" need not be about questions such as whether to "control" research, but about how we get to be thinking in those terms, as though the inevitability of research were to be taken as given.

RESPONSIBILITY

Oppenheimer, as we have seen, took a narrow view of the responsibility of the scientist "for the fruits of his work":

> . . . it must be clear to all of us how very modest such assumption of responsibility can be, how very ineffective it has been in the past, how necessarily ineffective it will surely be in the future. . . . The true responsibility of a scientist, as we all know, is to the integrity and vigor of his science.[12]

This was after Hiroshima. He must have known of an alternative, utilitarian, view in which the responsibility for actions might include their effects, however understood. A similar view can be reached from a more convincing route, where the ownership or authorship of what happens may not be so easily separable between intention and consequences. The appeal of a narrow view is clear enough, as are its conceptual connections with individual voluntary choice and personal accountability. At the narrowest extreme, there could be no responsibility for unintended consequences. This may seem preferable to the "sense of indeterminate guilt" that can be provoked as a consequence of a wider understanding,[13] but either extreme may stand as a reductio ad absurdum of a desire for excessive clarity. Little could be gained by trying to locate a "correct" point on a continuum between such extremes. At any time, courts of law may settle cases in which the extent of responsibility is in doubt; as Bernard Williams reminded us, this applies as significantly to the law of torts as to criminal liability.[14] But such settlements may be taken against a background of assumptions that may change. There may seem to be some allure in a historical relativism that suggests that the scope of responsibility has altered in the past and may alter again— and therefore that it has no "right" application—or that we are heirs to differing, conflicting concepts. Then, a solution might be to advocate a concept within some tradition that is preferred on wider grounds: the general strategy adopted by Alasdair MacIntyre in *After Virtue* and his subsequent writings. Or responsibility may be repudiated altogether, as "a word altogether devoid of signification and impossible of explanation," along the lines of Bradley in his essay on "The Vulgar Notion of Responsibility."[15]

There is no need to go quite so far to see the difficulties in the application of judgments about responsibility to Oppenheimer's choice in 1942. If he himself was hoping to limit his responsibility to "the integrity and vigor of his science" (since he was "not in a policy-making position at Los Alamos"[16]) he may have been too ambitious; but there may be genuine problems about where and how any judgment can be made. Bradley wrote that "subjection to a moral tribunal lies at the bottom of our answering for our deeds."[17] Less colorfully, we might consider the point of judgments about responsibility. From Oppenheimer's perspective, there seems to have been almost no point at all. He may have wanted to think that he had some duties toward what he saw as scientific values, but no responsibility beyond. Bradley's "moral tribunal" suggests the strong association between responsibility and answerability, presumably in some moral sense. His further suggestion was that such a moral sense was, at least, hard to pin down. The context for judgments is uncertain. As seen in chapter 5, in a legalistic sense we can take account of justification and mitigation and reach some verdict, but there are three serious problems.

First, there is the lack of symmetry between the factors relevant at Oppenheimer's point of choice—with what he could know then— and the factors known later, or now. His choice and our judgment seem too far apart. This might explain his caution about responsibility. It may seem reasonable to make a decision in the light of how it may be seen in hindsight, but not if you can have absolutely no idea of the extent of its effects.

Second, there is the lack of persuasiveness in the whole framework. Of course Oppenheimer was responsible to some large extent for the construction of the first atomic bombs. Others were responsible in other ways. Such judicious thoughts have no bearing on the less measured but no less certain way in which Oppenheimer said physicists had "known sin," or in which he felt he had blood on his hands, as he told Truman.[18] A legalistic appraisal may fail to capture what we may want from a notion of responsibility: which may be to conclude that this notion will not be pinned down without loss.

Third, we have to reflect on the legitimacy for our "moral tribunal." No doubt we feel entitled to hold opinions, in a sense of reacting favorably or otherwise. We may like to feel that our opinions matter, or even that we have some right to hold or express them. This is a point at which thinking about a specific question leads immediately to thinking about the point of moral thinking. If responsibility implies answerability, then to whom or what? Surely to more than our later opinions. God or the voice of conscience may be brought in if some sense of impersonal, objective moral arbitration seems too tenuous. Or a general responsibility to "the other" may be taken as primary, as it was for Levinas.[19] But in Oppenheimer's case that just takes us back unhelpfully to asking who the other would be. Present or future humanity in general? His country and its allies? His scientific colleagues?

These points will come up again shortly in a wider way. They might provide support for a Bradley in a view that responsibility is an example of conceptual failure in that it contains unsolvable contradictions, or exists in an unrealistically abstract context. Less severely, we may feel reluctant to deny our right to pass judgments on the responsibility for past decisions while at the same time feeling uncertain of our locus in such judgments: surely an uneasy priority for practical ethics over desirable reflection.

A NEW MORAL WORLD?

Chapter 6 looked at what might have seemed to be a different kind of conceptual failure: the supposed failure of existing moral concepts or frameworks to deal with the invention and development of the first atomic bombs. Much of this was not justifiable. Atomic weapons introduced some new factors, but these were quickly intelligible. The politics required to cope with atomic weapons turned out to be little different from politics in any other era. Fears, threats, interests, and power played their parts in ways that would have been grasped at once by Herodotus or Thucydides. This does not mean that the morality of the development and use of atomic weapons was well considered at the time. Hans Bethe admitted that he did not "pay much attention" to the moral problems created at Los Alamos during the war.[20] Oppenheimer's writings on the subject all date from later.

Insofar as there were specific problems created in "scientific ethics," these were not merely the result of conceptual inadequacy—as though the moral equipment to deal with machine guns, aerial bombardment, and submarines were unable to handle atomic bombs. Scientific change—or any historical, political, or social change—does create difficulties, but not of such a straightforward kind. Oppenheimer's choice in 1942—what he should do then—in the most trite sense was not the same as anyone else's choice at any other time. But the changed situation created in part by the outcome of his choice made it specific, or unique, in a less banal way. Once again, we see the disparity between his decision at the time and any later judgment—his or ours— on what he *should* have done. A timeless choice—with other things being equal—is not even a convenient but approximate artifice. It represents a distortion of the predicament in what could only be seen as a moral choice for a person, at a time, in a situation.

This is not to say that our—or his—later judgment would be invalidated. It means that the pretense of impersonality in representing some decisions may do more harm than good. We might like a moral *should* to be unambiguous—part of the Kantian hope for the purity of morality. The barrier between "What should I do?" and "What should I have done?" (or "What should he have done?") is not so easy to remove.

Scientific change may not create a new moral world but it may create a new world in which earlier decisions are particularly hard to appraise. In any situation the sheer unhelpfulness of asking "What should he have done?" can be significant. It is less plainly useless, but can be just as empty as "If only he had known." Scientific development, not uniquely, can make it impossible to have known.

PURITY

Another kind of challenge is presented by the issues raised in chapter 7. Straightforwardly, we may feel reluctant or unable to reach a view on Oppenheimer's contribution to what was an immense scientific-technical collaboration. Not because of a shortage of facts, but because we lack the compass to find our bearings. We know how to judge individual accountability for individual actions. The scale of the Manhattan Project, and its necessary amalgam of research with applied technology, may leave us unwilling to identify any point at which right or wrong can be assigned. Looking only at Oppenheimer as an individual, his decision to commit himself to Los Alamos in 1942–1943, while being crucial to the eventual outcome, might seem arbitrary as a focus for assessment or judgment. If he had decided otherwise, we might not be interested in him. Yet the gap between the initial step and the final explosions was far too uncertain for everything to rest on him and his choice. The central point is that we *can* resort to judgments on individual choices at specific times, but this only serves to show how poorly that approach captures what we may want to think.

One response may be that here we see further confirmation of how hard it can be to draw lessons from history. Things—people—events are just too complicated to allow for clear judgments on the past, and hence lessons for the future. Another may be, again, that our moral vocabulary is not sufficiently evolved to cover such developments. That is totally unpromising in leaving unresolved whether we are supposed to await the evolution of new moral vocabulary or to invent some for ourselves.

More radically, but also more convincingly, there may be some failure in description. Oppenheimer himself tried to take refuge at two poles: either in the uncorrupted purity and inexorability of science or in the modesty of his own practical contribution ("understanding, encouraging, suggesting and deciding"[21]). Different language (fathering, directing, ordering, organizing, building, making happen) contains differing implications in terms of responsibility. What is evident, and not surprising, is how much of the language used to characterize work like Oppenheimer's is tied to thinking on individual responsibility or accountability. This goes both ways, in that if we start by seeking to appraise his actions, we are more likely to think of direction and organization than of pure research or of encouragement. Where there is some failure it may be in our uncertainty in understanding rather than appraisal. Oppenheimer's own attempts at unprejudicial descriptions of his own work were not impressive. We do not know how far they were evasive.

This is a disturbing area, and no less so because it may seem so tenuous or vague. The whole point is that we find it easy—too easy—to think about the single act of an individual acting alone to produce a single outcome. But how much of life is like that? The Manhattan Project may be an extreme case of complexity, and we may find corresponding difficulty in thinking about it, or even about one individual's contribution. How much is that a result of the complexity, and how much a result of applying too simple a measure? The simple thought that agency or responsibility in a large collaborative project is the sum of individual responsibilities seems almost meaningless. The even simpler thought that agency or responsibility can be channeled in legal, constitutional, or bureaucratic terms to a single defined point does at least make sense, and may be convincing in some circumstances. But not much of life or thought can be so well ordered. In any event, this view is of no value if we are asking about the contribution of an individual. The difficult problem, after all, may be the point at which an individual can surrender responsibility to a group or hierarchy. The suggestion that "I was only obeying orders" could be a uniformly satisfactory defense is hardly convincing. The opposite extreme—of inalienable personal autonomy—is hardly practicable. Oppenheimer would have been willing to have served as a military officer at Los Alamos, but came to realize that this could not be acceptable to his scientific colleagues. Despite that attitude to hierarchy, he still ended the war with feelings of personal responsibility. In reply to Oppenheimer's remark about blood on his hands, Truman is reported to have said, "I told him the blood was on my hands—to let me worry about that."[22]

So, in the end, what do we want to say about Oppenheimer? At first sight, drama, biography, and psychological speculation all promise a richer seam of material than moral philosophy. On the other hand, drama or biography have no obligation to provide anything like answers. The rhetorical shrug of the shoulders can leave judgment to the audience or the reader. Paradoxes or inconsistencies between character and action or intentions and outcomes can be seen as interestingly tragic, or edifying, without any need to go further into the resolution or edification that might be inferred. There could be more to be learned about Oppenheimer's motivations before 1942, or after 1945, and this could cast some light on the security hearings of 1954. But this could not alter the record of his actions in taking up his post at Los Alamos and in building the first atomic bombs when he did.

Where is the place for a moral reaction, or for the moral philosopher, or even the moralist? One thought might be that moral reac-

tions have no place in history, which should be assembled in a judiciously neutral tone. Another might be that if a choice such as
Oppenheimer's, and the work he did, is not a field for moral consideration, then nothing is. Decisions such as his, to move into the
atomic weapons program in 1942, to continue with it after 1944, and
to defend it after 1945, may be seen as archetypal of what ethics or
morality is. Our view of his decisions—should he have done this?
should it have been done?—may be seen as archetypal of ethical or
moral judgments. This may be so despite the fact that it applies undeniably to a single person at a specific time. We know that questions
like: should it be done like that again? or: should he have chosen
otherwise? are some way from anything like an initial moral reaction—whatever that is—but we may still feel that we can learn something useful for ourselves and for the future. If not, why care at all?

Needless to say, the idea of "initial moral reactions" is not
uncontroversial. One of the fatal defects in the practical ethics movement is in the hope that we can try to answer moral questions without
too much reflection on the scope and nature of morality. (This may be
seen as a hardnosed preference for practice over "theory.") The problem
is that the scope of what is to count as moral can vary widely, often
itself as the result of moral argument. It is often pointed out that slavery
was simply not seen as a moral issue in the ancient world: it was just
a fact of existence like geography or the weather. More recently, as
noted in chapter 5,[23] suicide used to be regarded universally as appallingly
wicked. Kant appears to have regarded it as the very prototype of im-
morality, as a failure of duty to the self. That attitude no longer exists.
Although no one denies that suicide can be undesirable in various
ways, a moral way is seldom included. Psychiatry or social science su-
persedes morality. This is not a commonplace change in which something seen at one time or place as wrong is seen at another as right or
neutral. It is a real change in the scope of morality. We may frown in
disapproval at a man who kills himself leaving an unsupported widow,
a pile of debts, and sick children, but the idea that his suicide was
wrong "in itself" just seems puzzling.

Ironically, for the proponent of practical ethics, characteristically disposed toward utilitarianism, utilitarian moral assumptions may
have radical implications for the scope of morality. There is no need
to stray into theoretical debate to see this. It is easy to imagine a
military strategist appraising the options for a war, including of course

its medium and longer term effects. The strategist might be baffled to be asked whether "moral" considerations were being taken into account, or whether any weight was given to moral factors. In utilitarian terms, the whole calculation of injuries, profits, stability, chaos, deaths, collateral damage, power, and so on would *be* a moral calculation, without remainder. There could be no *extra* question of whether the planned warfare was right or wrong. This has two connected corollaries: a redrafting of the scope of morality and a refusal to regard some issues as moral.

The decision on the use of the first atomic bomb on Hiroshima can be presented like that. There could be calculations on immediate and future losses of life, where loss of life may be taken as an uncontroversial evil. The decision to drop the bomb on a crowded city could be seen—it has been seen—as the outcome of such calculation, where rightness or wrongness would not have been extra factors to be taken into account in the sums. The decision becomes removed from morality into political or military strategy. So there is nothing for the moral philosopher to consider.

That approach would have had advantages in easing the consciences of those who made the decision. The utilitarian can have no regrets. It still has undeniable appeal for the planners of warfare. If "moral factors" can be defined out of existence, then consideration of them can be seen as an unnecessary indulgence. The drawback lies in the initial characterization of a moral decision. If this is taken as the calculation of the least bad outcomes, against an agreed tariff of badness, then there is no difficulty. The point is not that we should not accept this—perhaps we might—but that it has to be defended against immediate objections, and so some level of argument about the nature of morality is unavoidable, and the mask of pure practicality peels away. If one protests that some decisions are wrong no matter what the outcomes, and the decision to torture is the usual example, it does not look productive to reply that torture can have some positive outcomes. The utilitarian moralist might accept a debate over whether torture is right or wrong, in the sense of the weight to be given to its immediate or wider effects. An opponent might refuse even to join such debate on the ground that right or wrong cannot be calculated in that way. The difference between the two would be about the scope of morality. In that it cannot be settled within the terms accepted by either side, this is normally taken as a contradiction within utilitarianism, where all moral differences are supposed to be calculable.

Anyway, regardless of theoretical discussion of whether moral reflection is possible, we may well feel that we have some *right* to a view: in this case, that there should be nothing stopping us from asking whether Oppenheimer chose correctly, and so on. Undoubtedly, we can *react*, in admiration, indifference, or distaste. Again, questions may press in. There are fundamental questions about rights and the kind of negative freedom seen here: yes, we *can* say what we feel and we may like doing this. Its elevation into a right seems to call for more thought. There is also the view that our reaction, or desire to react, is *all* there is: the reductivist view, in mid-twentieth-century fashion, that there is, or can be, "nothing more" to a judgment than a negative or positive reaction. (It is as though there is a trade-off: the price for the right to voice a moral reaction is that no reaction is worth more than any other.) There are well-trodden lines of dissent. Can a reaction really be purely self-directed, in the sense that something only makes *me*, or *us*, feel pleasant or disagreeable? Or must such feelings contain some reference to whatever provokes them?—something must be disagreeable *as* whatever it is. Then there is the implausibility of any engagement in debate. If one reaction is positive and another negative, is it really possible that no discussion of the grounds for the difference can be available? It is more than imaginable that someone could *feel* entirely unequivocal about Oppenheimer's decision in 1942—no feelings might be evoked except admiration and enthusiasm for his prompt response to the call of duty. Yet such feelings would still be directed towards qualities that themselves would have to be felt to be admirable, and so on. And a refusal to discuss whether a feeling of admiration was appropriate might seem dogmatic.

These are old debates. More pertinently, it can be asked who *we* are supposed to be in any moral appraisal. Not in any simple reaction of admiration or distaste, because such reactions are by their nature local and subjective. That cannot be in doubt. The difficult issue is of "our" place in anything purporting to be a moral judgment.

One purist view is that this issue cannot arise because a moral judgment is de facto nonpersonal. It is not anyone's judgment at any particular time. The very fact that such judgments are possible might be thought to be a vindication of morality in itself. This could have been Kant's view. The idea of the "point of view of the universe" was expanded by Henry Sidgwick from a different angle; and there can be a useful theoretical critique of this notion.[24] Keeping closer to the present discussion, there could be real qualms about the judgments, appraisals or simple opinions *we* may want to formulate, and about their function. On the one hand, it may seem more than fashionable piety to say that a judgment of Oppenheimer from a victim at Hiroshima or Nagasaki might differ from a judgment many years later in a country opposed to Japan in the Second World War. (And this kind of point is routine in discussions of the Nazi Holocaust, or of South African apartheid, where attitudes of past victims to commemoration, judgment, and forgiveness are often regarded as having special status.) On the other, there is a familiar view that it is exactly characteristic of moral judgments—in contrast with shifting historical interpretations, for example—that personal experiences can be held in abeyance. It may only beg the question to appeal to the neutrality of justice. There can be an ideal of justice, but also a kind of appropriate justice. (Are all juries the same? In a totally homogeneous society juries could be selected entirely at random; but not in the real world.) The kidnapping of Eichmann and his trial in Israel were affronts to international law; but the trial also represented the only available justice that fitted his case.

If the location of moral judgment may be open to question, what can be said about its function? In trying to apply some kind of moral appraisal to Oppenheimer's choice, what are we trying to *do*? Registering a judgment: but for what? The judgment might be taken formally, as universalizable and prescriptive—don't (or do) anything like that . . . although the realism of this was discussed in chapter 1. Nothing again will be *like that* and nobody will ever try to do it again.

We shall return shortly to the function or purpose of such judgments or appraisals. A problem to be kept in mind is the possible context. A legal verdict is passed in court. Divine judgment may take place in heaven. The contexts provide the location, legitimation, and function for the judgments. Plainly, moral verdicts can be assimilated both to legal and divine versions: the bar of history, the voice of conscience, the moral law, and so on. Can they be taken in any other way?

Leaving these reservations for the time being, what conclusions—or verdicts—can be reached by taking apart some of the strands in Oppenheimer's reflections after 1942? A few points do seem clear enough from chapters 3, 4, and 7, on values, curiosity, and on the purity of science.

First, Oppenheimer's dichotomy between "realities" for the scientist and "lights and values" for "mankind at large"[25] could not sustain the weight it had to carry. The way in which this dichotomy was used was overtly political, and also led itself to a particular view of politics and morality. Facts were for experts. When the facts were certain, decisions could be taken by others, presumably in some degree of uncertainty or relative ignorance. That approach may have looked necessary in the seventeenth century, when it may have been desirable to diminish the excessive dogmatism of politics—particularly theological politics. The Manhattan Project presents a stark example in which the space for moral choice and the space for factual certainties can be kept apart by definition, though it must be clear how artificial this can be. There is a link with previous points, on the scope and nature of morality. If a choice is for *someone* because those taking decisions are to be tidily separable from those delivering the facts, this may feel convenient for everyone, but there are good reasons to wonder why it should be acceptable. The question should be not to ask what is the alternative, but how this could be sustainable at all.

Second, the ideology of curiosity in research was not consistent with Oppenheimer's views on the separation of "realities" and values. The value of research is still a value. In particular, the thought that research must be pursued unless there is a reason why it should not would be exceptionally inappropriate to apply to the atomic bomb project: we did this job "because it was an organic necessity."[26] Political, financial, or moral necessity: perhaps so. Organic necessity or inevitability: no. Again, the alternative is not "control" of "science" by "politics" or "morality." The " " are all required because these terms do not *need* to be interdefined as they are, and the way they are taken here is at best tendentious.

Third, there are serious and difficult questions about the appraisal of the *kind* of work undertaken by Oppenheimer at Los Alamos. As seen in chapter 7, the organization of a large project fits awkwardly into our easiest models of assessment: who was in charge? who carried the can? What is less difficult to say is that the uncorrupted purity of science does not provide much shelter from appraisal, of whatever kind. How we *do* see the Manhattan Project is debatable. How we *cannot* see it is as a pure investigation of atomic physics, whether or not a great deal of new physics came out along the way.

In these three areas, judgments or verdicts seem possible. There are inconsistencies, and there are excuses that look plainly inadequate.

This is indeed judgmental, but it should be remembered that we are considering what in reality were not far from excuses or justifications offered by Oppenheimer after August 1945. The central apologia, quite overtly prepared in those terms, was in his farewell speech at Los Alamos in November 1945. Bluntly: giving poor excuses for what you have already done is not praiseworthy; but what about what had actually been done—the choice that had been made, and sustained, from 1942—actions not words?

و§

Here, things are less clear. From earlier in this chapter it can be seen that there are areas in which we have to be less confident in the place of anything like moral judgment on Oppenheimer's choice, in large part because of real uncertainty about the nature of morality itself. This is where we need to look at ourselves as much as at him, where reflection is required.

Four such areas came together, all discussed already at length. There is the notion of *authorship*—a kind of personal ownership of an action, in contrast with narrow causality. There is *acceptance*, in contrast with dissent as autonomy. There is the phenomenon conveyed in *no choice* but to act, Oppenheimer's "I do not think that the Nazis allow us the option,"[27] in contrast with an emphasis on unhampered freedom. Then there is corporate, shared, or *collective* responsibility, again in contrast with the clear choices of an individual. All of these offer problematic contrasts with clearly workable models of moral appraisal, and not as apologias or mitigations but as approaches from a different perspective. Instead of the individual, accountable for positively chosen single decisions, there is an alternative view of a personal contribution within real constraints, accepted as part of a hierarchy or team. If that looks like an opposition between heroic, individual activity and obedient passivity, then it should not. (There might be some shadow of stereotyped Protestant versus Catholic values in such a feeling, in an admiration for someone who strains to dissent alone, rather than to accept, concur, or submit.) Rather, one observation might be on the one-sidedness in the values that we may seem to be applying in our judgments. Here, the kinship between values and perspectives, argued by Nietzsche, is particularly apparent. What, for example, is the value in pressing the question, as though it were crucial: could he have said no? After all, we do not need to be reminded that, in one plain sense, Oppenheimer had a choice, and continued to have a choice. The reminder that is needed is that in another sense he may have felt that he had none. The significance of that should not be undervalued.

≈∮

More widely, as seen many times in this study, the easiest model to apply is one of legalistic appraisal: a well-established framework for ascribing responsibility where individual choice, freedom, and agency can be balanced against recognized excuses or mitigations. Equally, the model of appraisal itself may be legalistic: we *judge* a choice. That need not imply guilt or blame, but the thought may be one of framing a judgment with a legal-moral verdict. And further, of course, this also offers a ready model for morality itself, cutting through some of the hesitations that may unsettle our feelings about its nature: the "moral law." Once again, there could be a shadow from religion. We presume to judge morally—impartially, judiciously—as God was supposed to judge. The human eye can never see everything clearly and fairly, and the human mind can never judge without some prejudice, but the eye and mind of God can serve as models of objectivity, even if seen as wholly suppositional. (That, at least, can be one religious model. There can also be another, placing emphasis antinomially on grace or mercy rather than on law and justice. The same biblical story, of the sacrifice of Isaac, could be read in diametrically opposite senses. Kant saw it as an appalling affront to the moral law: Abraham should have paid attention to the voice of his own conscience, which would have told them that any other voice would be delusional.[28] Kierkegaard, at great length in *Fear and Trembling*, thought that it was exactly in the transcendence of the law that true morality was revealed.)

It would surely be a thankless task to argue that any of these models is right or wrong, whatever that would imply. It is not even easy to think about which "fits the facts" as we hope them to be. If we assume—as Nietzsche argued that we do—that we do have some preconception of "our morality," then a strictly law-governed, judicial template will not fit. We know, for example, that almost everyone will give priority to personal or family partiality, and feel no reservation about this, in preference to a more just distribution of affection, care, or resources. One routine response can be that such feelings may be real but cannot embody real morality just because that has to be impartial in important ways. In other words, the model is not descriptive but stipulative or prescriptive. And we *ought* to accept it because obligation itself can only be understood morally—and so on.

If such deadlock seems hard to break, the facts in the case might be relevant. Naturally (in view of the Allied victory) there was never any question of a legal appraisal of Oppenheimer's decision to start work on the bomb in 1942 or the rightness of his continuation with it until 1945. The only sense that could be extracted from a legal model would be along the lines of some moral law "higher" than the laws and constitution of his country, against which we might seek to form a judgment of him. (This need not be so detached from reality. A parallel: Edward Teller received the most intense disapproval of many former colleagues for what they saw as his betrayal of Oppenheimer at the 1954 hearings. Their judgment was not that he had acted against any law except "laws" of loyalty, decency, and friendship.) But, as we have seen, there are genuine difficulties in agreeing on which principles (or "moral laws") Oppenheimer might have observed or broken, and at what point. The need for endless qualifications—a scientist should not work on armaments *except . . .*—seems insuperable.

Our position is important because our presumption to make a judgment, or pass a verdict, can be questioned directly. Not a few historians argue that they should not make moral judgments on the past, but seek only to interpret and understand. The issue of pure interpretation was aired in chapter 5. (A corollary might be that only limited lessons for the future may be drawn from the past.) A reductio ad absurdum of that view might point out that most judgments can be seen as being about the past, and it seems excessive to say that we cannot pass verdicts on actions yesterday, last week, or last year; so why not last century?

This matters in that the ground or location—spatial metaphor seems unavoidable—for moral judgments can be so contestable. Local or national differences could be significant. The U.S. Constitution, for example, as understood in practice in the late twentieth century, was taken to mean that what could be seen as moral issues—of ethnic fairness in education, or abortion, say—were arbitrated not by politicians in Congress but by judges in the Supreme Court. Skeptics from less legally inclined lands might point out that the judges were nonetheless appointed by politicians (and the 2000 presidential election added a further twist to this spiral). Clearly, many practical and historical factors are relevant, but one theoretical thought is that apparently moral conflicts may be seen as judiciable, against a background of precedent and experience: questions can be given answers. But how far this stops anyone from asking further questions, or pressing further debate, is less obvious. What look like attempts to find a site where moral conflict can be resolved both impartially and decisively may not be finally successful. Maybe a lawyer would say that all legal debate has to be continuing.

Our position in forming what we take to be moral judgments on a past decision can be questioned in another way. There is a gap, which has come up several times in this study, between a subjective point of decision—what shall I do next?—and a judgment on that decision—was that done rightly, by me or another? Some would like that gap to close, as where choice of what to do next is not merely informed by the prospect of external judgment, by me (later) or another (now or later), but where this becomes the central element in any choice. As we have seen, this may not be possible, and not only because of luck and the unpredictability of events. The conclusion would be that a question like what should I do? may be unavoidable, whereas a question like what should I, or he, have done? may not be answerable. In Oppenheimer's case, a simple judgment might be: he should have said no. Which implies that we think he ought to have chosen other than he did. Plainly, we can *say* that. The trouble is not so much one of entitlement to say it, as in the point we think it has, apart from just voicing an opinion. I. I. Rabi chose in 1942 not to accept work at Los Alamos (though he changed his position later). Joseph Rotblat chose to leave Los Alamos in 1944 when he came to believe the work was no longer justified by the war in Europe. So, similarly, Oppenheimer could have chosen not to work at Los Alamos or to leave in 1944? In one way, of course. In another, he was neither Rabi nor Rotblat, and the responsibilities he was asked to accept and to bear were not the same as theirs. The emphasis on what *he* should or could have done is neither a concession to determinism nor to the predominance of internal reasons, or personal motives, over external reasons. It should alert us to the limits in our scope for judgment, in the limits for autonomous judgment.

Some of the strands disentangled in this book should have clear enough implications. There were evident shortcomings in Oppenheimer's reflections on values and science, and on the purity and inevitability of research. These can be seen as rationalizations after his work at Los Alamos was complete. Yet even if they are only taken as excuses, their frailty is worth seeing. They should not be used again.

It should not be surprising or frustrating that so decisive a conclusion cannot follow as a final verdict on his actions or on his initial choice in 1942. As suggested by the quotation from Kant at the beginning of this chapter, it is easy enough to have opinions and still easier to express feelings, but less easy to find what Kant called "grounds." The trouble is that there can be a variety of different grounds, some of which may serve to unsettle initial opinions or feelings. The step from thinking about Oppenheimer to thinking about thinking about Oppenheimer—to reflection, or moral philosophy—is short and unavoidable. There are ways in which a "verdict" on him can be delivered unproblematically. By the laws and constitution of his country what he did was unquestionably legal. It was, and still is, praised by many. Technically, his work was successful. As he said himself, "It is also alleged to have helped end the war,"[29] and, if that is correct, then it was a military success. But when—or if—we ask how far his work, or his decision to enter into it, was commendable in other ways, we have seen how quickly questions multiply. Only to start: *what* other ways? commendable *by or to whom*? within what context?

Again, some measure of clarity can be achieved by trying to sort out the various expectations we may have from our reflections, from the diverse questions considered by moral philosophers. We find questions about what to do next: decisions on right or wrong. There are questions about what is to be admired and commended: views on goodness. There is general guidance on how to live: values or moral perspectives. There are models for character, or virtues and vices. In addition, we may hope to make judgments on all of these: as well as deciding what to do, what to admire, how to live, what to emulate, we may try to determine how well these have been attained. Further, we may hope to answer demands of consistency and justification, not necessarily to the extent of rationalization in a bad sense but at least as far as being able to avoid contradictions and answer criticism. More ambitiously, we may hope to be able to characterize what we think we are doing. And from all this we may seek to extract guidance, or lessons, on what to do, how to live, and so on.

In looking at Oppenheimer, we can see that such expectations can only be met to some degree. Centrally, there should have been evident discordance between his decision on what to do in 1942—and we need not even mention rightness or morality, just what to do—and any judgment later on his choice. There is also a distinct unhelpfulness about any notion of character (or virtue). At the point when Oppenheimer decided to work at Los Alamos, atomic physics had been a harmless and almost entirely theoretical pursuit. His choice, in some sense, arose from who and what he was then, but we have seen how uneasily a point of choice, or responsibility, can be located.

In seeking to characterize what we think *we* are doing—in the step from opinion to reflection—we run into the obstacle identified by Nietzsche. Morality cannot be taken as "given." Oppenheimer's choice can be seen as nothing whatever to do with morality: the legality and the technical-military success exhaust any scope for appraisal. Or—more or less the same—any further appraisal is only a matter of personal opinion. From the other direction, it could be insisted once more that if such a choice is not a moral one, then nothing is; that this is archetypally what morality is. Both extremes may be asserted genuinely, with some force. The difference between them means that a characterization of morality is not optional. Attempts to narrow morality to a point where Oppenheimer's decision would be excluded seem likely to be arbitrary and unimpressive.

Some of the ways in which Oppenheimer saw himself as a scientist needed more support. He made no claim to be a moral philosopher, but some important elements in his defense of his work were not strong enough to bear the weight put on them. Some of the ways in which we see him, and the values or perspectives we apply, need attention, too. We have readily at hand the tools for the judgment of individual personal accountability; and it has to be stressed that in many cases these tools may fit and may work. Where they fit is another matter. In many cases, it would require unwarranted skepticism to question this. But what if we are reflecting on a decision—a moral choice—when these tools do not seem to fit: where we find the acceptance and ownership of a course of action as a point in the life of a person, and as part of a large endeavor? Here, the seat of judgment should feel less comfortable.

NOTES

ABBREVIATIONS

L = Smith, Alice Kimball, and Weiner, Charles. *Robert Oppenheimer: Letters and Recollections*. Stanford: Stanford University Press, 1995.

M = Stoff, M. B., Fanton, J. F., and Williams, R. H. *The Manhattan Project: A Documentary Introduction to the Atomic Age*. Philadelphia: Temple University Press, 1991.

T = United States Atomic Energy Commission. In the Matter of J. Robert Oppenheimer: Transcript of Hearing Before Personnel Security Board, Washington DC, April 12, 1954, through May 6, 1954. Washington DC: U.S. Government Printing Office, 1954.

INTRODUCTION

1. See Alice Kimball Smith, *A Peril and a Hope: The Scientists' Movement in America, 1945–1947*. Chicago: University of Chicago Press, 1965.

2. For example, recently, S. S. Schweber, *In the Shadow of the Bomb: Oppenheimer, Bethe, and the Responsibility of the Scientist*. Princeton: Princeton University Press, 2000. The most detailed study of the work at Los Alamos is Lillian Hoddeson, Paul W. Henriksen, Roger A Meade, Catherine Westfall et al., *Critical Assembly: A Technical History of Los Alamos during the Oppenheimer Years, 1943–1945*. Cambridge: Cambridge University Press, 1993.

3. Roger Robb, counsel for the AEC Personnel Security Board, cross-questioning Oppenheimer, April 16, 1954, T, p. 235.

4. Questioning by Lloyd K. Garrison, Oppenheimer's lawyer, April 15, 1954, T, pp. 163, 165.

5. Leslie R. Groves, *Now It Can be Told: The Story of the Manhattan Project*. London: Deutsch, 1963, pp. 413–414, 63.

6. For example, very critically, Paul Lawrence Ross, *Heisenberg and the Nazi Atomic Bomb Project: A Study in German Culture*. Berkeley: University of California Press, 1998.

7. Andrei Sakharov, *Memoirs*, trans. Richard Lourie. New York: Knopf, 1990, p. 96.

8. I. I. Rabi et al., *Oppenheimer*. New York: Scribner's, 1969, p. 8.

9. Theodor Adorno and Max Horkheimer, *Dialectic of Enlightenment* (1944), trans. John Cumming. London: Verso, 1995.

10. L, p. 316.

11. David Hawkins, *Manhattan District History: Project Y: The Los Alamos Project*, vol. 1, *Inception until August 1945*. Los Alamos: Los Alamos Scientific Laboratory Report LAMS-2532, vol. 1, December 1, 1961 (reprinted with a new Introduction, Los Angeles/San Francisco: Tomash, 1983).

12. See Smith, *A Peril and a Hope*, and M, Part 4.

13. Groves, *Now It Can Be Told*, p. 415.

14. *Metaphysics* A1, 980a (the opening words); Augustine, *Confessions* X, xxxv (54).

15. L, p. 317.

16. "Physics in the Contemporary World," *Bulletin of the Atomic Scientists*, 4 no. 3, 1948, p. 66.

17. Groves, *Now It Can Be Told*, Appendix VIII, p. 437, and M, p. 191.

18. *Operation Epsilon: The Farm Hall Transcripts*. Bristol and Philadelphia: Institute of Physics Publishing, 1993, report by Major T. H. Rittner, August 6–7, 1945, p. 70.

19. *Memoirs*, p. 96.

CHAPTER 1

1. In *Practical Philosophy*, trans. and ed. Mary J. Gregor. Cambridge: Cambridge University Press, 1996, pp. 593, 63.

2. L, p. 140.

3. Samuel Johnson, *The Life of Mr. Richard Savage* (1744), in *Johnson: Prose and Poetry*, ed. Mona Wilson. London: Hart-Davis, 1970, p. 118.

4. Gitta Sereny, *Into that Darkness* (1974). London: Pimlico, 1995, p. 367.

5. Summation by Oppenheimer's lawyer, Lloyd K. Garrison, May 6, 1954, T, p. 990.

6. *Practical Philosophy*, p. 65.

7. Iris Murdoch, "The Idea of Perfection" (1962), in *Existentialists and Mystics*, ed. Peter Conradi. London: Chatto and Windus, 1997, p. 323.

8. *The Gay Science* (1882/1887), trans. Josefine Nauckhoff. Cambridge: Cambridge University Press, 2001, IV, §335, p. 189.

9. Albert R. Jonsen and Stephen Toulmin, *The Abuse of Casuistry: A History of Moral Reasoning*. Berkeley: University of California Press, 1988, p. 330.

10. Starting, for example, from Nagel's "War and Massacre" and Hare's "Rules of War and Moral Reasoning," both in *Philosophy and Public Affairs*, 1, 2, 1972, and running at least to articles in Nagel's *Other Minds* (Oxford: Oxford University Press, 1995). See also papers in *Moral Particularism*, eds. Brad Hooker and Margaret Little. Oxford: Clarendon Press, 2000.

11. *Groundwork*, in *Practical Philosophy*, pp. 44–45.

12. *Critique of Pure Reason*, A811–B839.

13. *Practical Philosophy*, p. 163. The example draws on "The Creed of a Savoyard Priest" in Rousseau's *Émile*.

14. *The Conflict of the Faculties* (1798), in *Religion and Rational Theology*, trans. and ed. Allen W. Wood and G. di Giovanni. Cambridge: Cambridge University Press, 1996, p. 283n.

15. Bernard Williams, *Ethics and the Limits of Philosophy*. London: Fontana, 1985, p. 195.

16. *Critique of Practical Reason*, p. 164, and *The Metaphysic of Morals*, p. 560, in *Practical Philosophy*.

17. "Reason and Politics in the Kantian Enterprise" (also "The power of example"), in *Constructions of Reason*. Cambridge: Cambridge University Press, 1989, p. 21.

18. For example, recently, Ted Honderich, *Philosopher: A Kind of Life*. London: Routledge, 2001, ch. 19.

19. *Culture and Value*, ed. G. H. von Wright, trans. Peter Winch. Oxford: Blackwell, 1984, p. 34 (1938); p. 80 (1949).

CHAPTER 2

1. L, p. 250. See John S. Rigden, *Rabi: Scientist and Citizen*. New York: Basic Books, 1987, pp. 151–153, 216–217.

2. Robert Jungk, *Brighter than a Thousand Suns* (1956), trans. James Cleugh. Harmondsworth: Penguin, 1960, p. 119; Edward Teller, *Memoirs*. Cambridge: Perseus, 2001, pp, 162, 378.

3. L, p. 140.

4. Quoted in Schweber, *In the Shadow of the Bomb*, p. 215n70 (interview with Schweber, July 1992).

5. Oppenheimer: "Autobiographical Sketch," 1954, reprinted in M, p. 32 and T, p. 13.

6. A short review of controversy surrounding Heisenberg was given by Max Perutz in "Why Did the Germans Not Make the Bomb?," in *I Wish I'd Made You Angrier Earlier*. Oxford: Oxford University Press, 1998.

7. Thomas Nagel, "Moral Luck" (1976), in *Mortal Questions*. Cambridge: Cambridge University Press, 1979, p. 34.

8. Richard Rorty, "On Heidegger's Nazism," in *Philosophy and Social Hope*. London: Penguin, 1999, p. 196; see also Nagel, "Moral Luck," pp. 26, 34.

9. The inference analyzed by G. E. Moore in "Certainty," in *Philosophical Papers*. London: Allen & Unwin, 1959, pp. 231–233.

10. *Shame and Necessity*. Berkeley: University of California Press, 1993, p. 69.

11. April 16, 1954, T, p. 236.

12. Epictetus, *Discourses*, trans. E. Carter, revised R. Hard. London: Everyman, 1995, 1, 2, 12–14.

13. Vladimir Bukovsky, *To Build a Castle*. London: Deutsch, 1978, p. 80.

14. One historian has described the saying ascribed to Luther as "the motto of all Protestants—ultimately, perhaps, of all western civilization," Diarmaid MacCulloch, *Reformation: Europe's House Divided 1490–1700*. London: Allen Lane, 2003, p. 131.

15. See Williams, *Shame and Necessity*, pp. 59–60.

16. Hannah Arendt, *Eichmann in Jerusalem*. Harmondsworth: Penguin, 1976, p. 294.

17. Adam Smith, *The Theory of Moral Sentiments* (1759), eds. D. D. Raphael and A. L. Macfie. Indianapolis: Liberty Fund reprint, 1984, II, p. iii.

18. Quoted in Schweber, *In the Shadow of the Bomb*, p. 166.

CHAPTER 3

1. L, p. 317.

2. *The Legacy of Hiroshima*, with Allen Brown (Garden City: Doubleday, 1962), pp. 13–14 (quoted in L, p. 56); also, more negatively—well after Oppenheimer's death—*Memoirs*, pp. 206, 380.

3. M, p. 150.

4. "Encouragement of Science," *Bulletin of the Atomic Scientists*, January 1951, p. 7.

5. Quoted in Nuel Pharr Davis, *Lawrence and Oppenheimer*. London: Cape, 1969, p. 186.

6. Bernard Williams, "Morality, Scepticism and the Nuclear Arms Race," in N. Blake and K. Pole, eds., *Objections to Nuclear Defence*. London: Routledge, 1984, p. 100.

7. "Atomic Weapons," *Proceedings of the American Philosophical Society*, 90, no. 1, 1946 (address November 16, 1945), pp. 8, 9; see Mary Tiles and Hans Oberdiek, *Living in a Technological Culture*. London: Routledge, 1995, pp. 54–61.

8. See pp. 30 above; T, p. 236.

9. One exotic theory is elaborated by James A. Hijiya in "The Gita of J. Robert Oppenheimer," *Proceedings of the American Philosophical Society*, 144, no. 2, June 2000.

10. Lawrence Badash, *Scientists and the Development of Nuclear Weapons*. Atlantic Highlands, NJ: Humanities Press, 1995, p. 61.

11. Richard Feynman, *The Meaning of It All*. London: Allen Lane, 1998, pp. 43–45.

12. Ernest Gellner, *Language and Solitude: Wittgenstein, Malinowski and the Habsburg Dilemma*. Cambridge: Cambridge University Press, 1998, pp. 91–92.

13. Emmanuel Levinas, *Autrement qu'être ou au-delà de l'essence*. Paris: Livres de Poche, 1978, p. 195.

14. Cambridge: Cambridge University Press, 1989.

15. Emmanuel Levinas, *Totalité et Infini*. Paris: Livres de Poche, 1971, p. 37; also pp. 33, 89.

16. Richard Feynman, Minority Report to the Space Shuttle *Challenger* Inquiry, in *The Pleasure of Finding Things Out*. London: Allen Lane, 2000, p. 169.

17. *Totalité et Infini*, pp. 5, 245.

18. *Critique of Pure Reason*, A829–830=B857–858.

19. Jonathan Glover, *Humanity: A Moral History of the Twentieth Century* (London: Cape, 1999, p. 103) and *Responsibility* (London: Routledge and Kegan Paul, 1970, p. 180), quoting from Jungk, *Brighter than a Thousand Suns*, p. 292.

CHAPTER 4

1. L, p. 317; "Atomic Weapons," p. 7.

2. *Now It Can be Told*, p. 140.

3. Edward Teller, "Atomic Scientists Have Two Responsibilities," *Bulletin of the Atomic Scientists*, 3 no. 12, 1947, p. 356.

4. J. Robert Oppenheimer, "The Sciences and Man's Community" (1953), in *Atom and Void*. Princeton: Princeton University Press, 1989, p. 75.

5. L, p. 317.

6. Joseph Rotblat, "Leaving the Bomb Project," *Bulletin of the Atomic Scientists*, 41, no.7, August 1985, p. 18.

7. *Confessions*, trans. Henry Chadwick. Oxford: Oxford University Press, 1992, X, xxxv (54) and V, iv (7), pp. 210–211 and 75.

8. *Being and Time* (1927), trans. Joan Stambaugh, Albany: State University of New York Press, 1996, §36.

9. Nicolas Malebranche, *The Search after Truth* (1674/5), trans. T. M. Lennon. Cambridge: Cambridge University Press, Book IV, ch. 3, p. 278.

10. *Philosophical Writings*, trans. J. Cottingham, R. Stoothoff, D. Murdoch. Cambridge: Cambridge University Press, 1985, I, pp. 180, 184, 189.

11. *The Gay Science*, III, §123, p. 180.

12. *The Search after Truth*, p. 279.

13. Trans. S. Shirley. Indianapolis: Hackett, 1992, §13, p. 233.

14. *Ethics*, trans. S. Shirley. Indianapolis: Hackett, 1992, IV, Proposition 28 and IV, Appendix, 4.

15. *Ethics*, Preface to Part III.

16. *Discourse on the Method*, V, in *Philosophical Writings*, I, p. 141.

17. *Republic*, trans. G. M. A. Grube, rev. C. D. C. Reeve, in *Complete Works*, ed. J. M. Cooper. Indianapolis: Hackett, 1997, VI, 490ab.

18. *A Treatise of Human Nature*, 2.3.10, "Of curiosity, or the love of truth," §4.

19. *On the Genealogy of Morality* (1887), trans. Keith Ansell-Pearson. Cambridge: Cambridge University Press, 1994, III, §24, p. 120.

20. *The Gay Science*, V, §344, p. 281; III, §123.

21. *On the Genealogy of Morality*, III, §24, p. 119.

22. *The Gay Science*, III, §123, p. 178.

23. *On the Genealogy of Morals*, III, §25, p. 120.

24. *The Gay Science*, V, §344, pp. 281–283. The interpretation follows Maudmarie Clark, *Nietzsche on Truth and Philosophy*. Cambridge: Cambridge University Press, 1990, pp. 180–203.

25. An important theme in Bernard Williams, *Truth and Truthfulness*. Princeton: Princeton University Press, 2002.

26. Stephen Toulmin, *Cosmopolis*. Chicago: University of Chicago Press, 1992.

27. Michel de Montaigne, *An Apology for Raymond Sebond* (1569), trans. M. A. Screech. Harmondsworth: Penguin, 1987.

28. For example, *Thus Spoke Zarathustra* (1883/1885), trans. R. J. Hollingdale. Harmondsworth: Penguin, 1969, "Of the Thousand and One Goals," pp. 84–86.

CHAPTER 5

1. Notes of the Interim Committee Meeting, Thursday, May 31, 1945, in M, p. 117.

2. For example, John Martin Fischer and Mark Ravizza, *Responsibility and Control: A Theory of Moral Responsibility*. Cambridge: Cambridge University Press, 1998.

3. Interview with Studs Terkel, *Guardian*, August 6, 2002.

4. See Elazar Barkan, *The Guilt of Nations: Restitution and Negotiating Historical Injustices*. New York: Norton, 2000.

5. "Collective Responsibility," in *Responsibility and Judgment*. New York: Schocken, 2003, p. 147.

6. "Physics in the Contemporary World," p. 67.

7. *Metaphysics of Morals*, I, Part I.

8. "Modern Moral Philosophy," *Philosophy*, 33, 1958.

9. *Sources of the Self*, chs. 1 and 2. Hume, "Of the Standard of Taste" (1741), in *Essays*. Oxford: Oxford University Press, 1963, pp. 233–234.

10. *History of England*, vol. II, ch. 23, end.

11. Richard J. Evans, *In Defence of History*. London: Granta, 1997, p. 52.

12. *Political Treatise*, trans. S. Shirley. Indianapolis: Hackett, 2000, I, 4.

13. "Ruthlessness in Public Life," in Nagel, *Mortal Questions*; Peter A. French, *Collective and Corporate Responsibility*. New York: Columbia University Press, 1984.

14. See T, p. 28.

15. "The Vulgar Notion of Responsibility" (1876), in *Ethical Studies*. Oxford: Oxford University Press, 1970.

16. "Codes, and the Arrangement of the Law," *American Law Review*, 5, no. 1, 1870, in S. M. Novick, ed., *Collected Works of Justice Holmes*. Chicago: University of Chicago Press, 1995, vol. 1, pp. 212–213.

17. Kant, *Groundwork*, in *Practical Philosophy*, pp. 73–74, 80; *Lectures on Ethics*, Peter Heath and J. B. Schneewind, eds. Cambridge: Cambridge University Press, 1997, pp. 144–149; Hume, "Of Suicide," in *Essays*.

18. *An Enquiry concerning the Principles of Morals* (1751), ed. Tom L. Beauchamp. Oxford: Oxford University Press, 1998, Appendix 4, §21.

19. Minutes of the President's Meeting of June 18, 1945, in M, p. 152.

20. See M, Parts 3 and 5.

21. See French, *Collective and Corporate Responsibility*, ch. 8.

22. Emmanuel Levinas, *Autrement qu'être, ou au-delà de l'essence*, pp. 186–189; also "Sans identité" in *L'humanisme de l'autre homme* (1978), Paris: Livres de Poche, n.d., pp. 110–111.

23. Václav Havel, *Letters to Olga*, trans. Paul Wilson. London: Faber and Faber, 1990, pp. 266, 323 (Letters of 1982). See also Jan Patočka, *Heretical Essays in the Philosophy of History*, Erazim Kohák, trans. Chicago: Open Court, 1996, p. 107.

CHAPTER 6

1. M, p. 267; Groves *Now It Can be Told*, p. 253.

2. See Paul Boyer, *By the Bomb's Early Light: American Thought and Culture at the Dawn of the Atomic Age*. New York: Pantheon Books, 1985, ch. 1 ("The whole world gasped").

3. "Physics in the Contemporary World," p. 86.

4. See Donald MacKenzie with Graham Spinardi, "Tacit Knowledge and the Uninvention of Nuclear Weapons," in D. MacKenzie, *Knowing Machines: Essays on Technical Change*. Cambridge: MIT Press, 1996.

5. Vannevar Bush, *Modern Arms and Free Men*. London: Heinemann, 1950, p. 101.

6. A sizeable literature weighs up the uniqueness of the Nazi Holocaust; for example, Emil L. Fackenheim, "The Holocaust and Philosophy," *Journal of Philosophy*, 82/10, October 1985.

7. See page 9.

8. Victor F. Weisskopf, "The Los Alamos Years," in Rabi et al., *Oppenheimer*, pp. 24, 27; Mary McCarthy, letter to *Politics*, November 1946, p. 367.

9. In *The American Atom: A Documentary History of Nuclear Policies from the Discovery of Nuclear Fission to the Present 1939–1984*, Robert C. Williams and Philip L. Cantelon, eds. Philadelphia: University of Pennsylvania Press, 1984, p. 18.

10. P. M. S. Blackett, *Military and Political Consequences of Atomic Energy*. London: Turnstile Press, 1948 (in United States: *Fear, War, and the Bomb*), p. 127.

11. April 16, 1954, T, p. 250.

12. See Martin J. Sherwin, *A World Destroyed: The Atomic Bomb and the Grand Alliance* (New York: Knopf, 1975) and Gar Alperovitz, *Atomic Diplomacy* (London: Secker & Warburg, 1966); such allegedly "revisionist" arguments are reviewed briefly in Paul Boyer, *Fallout*. Columbus: Ohio State University Press, 1998, ch. 16. A different utilitarian argument is used by Michael Walzer, in *Just and Unjust Wars*. New York: Basic Books, 2nd ed., 1992, pp. 266–268.

13. See Boyer, *By the Bomb's Early Light*, ch. 9 ("The Scientists' Movement in Eclipse").

14. Vivid testimony is given in W. G. Sebald, *On the Natural History of Destruction*, trans. Anthea Bell. London: Hamish Hamilton, 2003.

15. In Williams and Cantelon, *The American Atom*, p. 68.

16. Jürgen Habermas, "The scientization of politics and public opinion," from *Technik und Wissenschaft als 'Ideologie,'* Frankfurt: Suhrkamp Verlag, 1968, trans. J. J. Shapiro in *Toward a Rational Society*. London: Heinemann, 1971, pp. 78–79.

17. Williams and Cantelon, *The American Atom*, p. 69.

18. G. H. Hardy, *A Mathematician's Apology* (1940). Cambridge: Cambridge University Press, 1992, p. 140.

19. September 1945, quoted in Boyer, *By the Bomb's Early Light*, p. 14; draft letter to Eden, March 25, 1945 (the second passage was excised in the final version), from M, p. 87.

20. New York: St Martin's Press, 1995.

21. Oppenheimer hearings, April 19 and 27, 1954, T, pp. 326 and 649–650. Von Neumann was also talking about the security problems at Los Alamos.

22. "Atomic Weapons," p. 8.

23. Diary notes of Secretary Henry L. Stimson, Sunday, July 22, 1945, in M, p. 205; I. I. Rabi quoted in Richard Rhodes, *The Making of the Atomic Bomb*. Harmondsworth: Penguin, 1986, p. 676 (from a television interview in 1980, KTEH-TV, San Jose, CA).

24. *An Enquiry concerning the Principles of Morals*, 5, §13.

25. *Critique of Practical Reason*, in Gregor, *Practical Philosophy*, p. 219.

26. For example, hearing on April 13, 1954, T, pp. 78–80.

27. Thomas Nagel, *The Last Word*. New York: Oxford, 1997, p. 119.

28. For example, Williams, in *Ethics and the Limits of Philosophy*, ch. 10.

29. April 16, 1954, T, p. 229.

30. Bernard Williams, "Internal and external reasons," in *Moral Luck*. Cambridge: Cambridge University Press, 1981.

31. *An Essay concerning Human Understanding*, II, 27, §26.

32. *Critique of Pure Reason*, A554–555=B582–583.

33. *The Theory of Moral Sentiments*, III, 1, p. 113.

34. *The Last Word*, p. 120.

35. *Critique of Pure Reason*, A553=B581.

36. See p. 9 above (Groves, *Now It Can be Told*, Appendix VIII, p. 437 and M, p. 191).

CHAPTER 7

1. L, p. 316.

2. "Creators of the Bomb"(Review of Schweber, *In the Shadow of the Bomb*), *New York Review of Books*, May 11, 2000.

3. See p. 94n4 above.

4. "The Los Alamos Years," in Rabi et al., *Oppenheimer*, pp. 24–25.

5. Letter to Maj. Gen. K. D. Nichols, March 4, 1954, T, p. 14.

6. *Nicomachean Ethics*, VI, 5, 1140b24.

7. "Physics in the Contemporary World," p. 67.

8. Speech at Los Alamos, November 2, 1945, L, p. 317.

9. *Atom and Void*, p. 75.

10. *Responsibility*, p. 180.

11. Philip Kitcher, *Science, Truth, and Democracy*. Oxford: Oxford University Press, 2001, pp. 80, 89; Martin Heidegger, *The Question Concerning Technology* (1950), Willam Lovitt, trans., New York: Harper, 1977, pp. 12–14.

12. "Physics in the Contemporary World," p. 67.

13. Hoddeson et al., *Critical Assembly*, p. 5.

14. L, p. 317.

15. "Heisenberg, Oppenheimer, and Modern Physics" in *The Advancement of Science, and Its Burdens*. Cambridge: Cambridge University Press, 1986, p. 160.

16. See Keith Graham, *Practical Reasoning in a Social World*. Cambridge: Cambridge University Press, 2002, ch. 3.

17. See p. 101 above.

18. Recently, Mark Lilla, *The Reckless Mind: Intellectuals in Politics*. New York: NYRB, 2001.

19. Robert Skidelsky, *John Maynard Keynes*. London: Macmillan, 2000, vol. 3, p. 140; John Maynard Keynes, *The General Theory of Employment, Interest and Money* (1936). London: Macmillan, 1964, p. 383.

20. Teller, "Atomic Scientists Have Two Responsibilities," p. 356 (see p. 56).

21. From II, 368c.

22. Habermas, "The scientization of politics and public opinion," pp. 63–64.

23. Ferdinand Tönnies, *Community and Civil Society* (1887), trans. Jose Harris. Cambridge: Cambridge University Press, 2001, pp. 132, 96, 138–140.

24. See, for example, Raymond Geuss, *Public Goods, Private Goods*. Princeton: Princeton University Press, 2001.

25. The classic text is chapter XX of Spinoza's *Theological-Political Treatise*.

26. Teller, *Memoirs*, p. 171.

27. Bernstein, "Creators of the Bomb."

28. R. M. Hare, *Freedom and Reason*. Oxford: Oxford University Press, 1963, p. 15.

29. April 16, 1954, T, p. 236.

30. April 27, 1954, T, p. 650; see p. 105.

31. G. E. M. Anscombe, *Intention*. Oxford: Blackwell, 1957, §47.

32. See p. 30.

33. Jeremy Bernstein, *Hitler's Uranium Club: The Secret Recordings at Farm Hall*. Woodbury NY: American Institute of Physics, 1996, p. 120ff.

34. Rotblat, "Leaving the bomb project."

35. For example, chapters in Aleksandar Jokic, ed., *War Crimes and Collective Wrongdoings*. Oxford: Blackwell, 2001.

CHAPTER 8

1. In *Theoretical Philosophy 1755–1770*, trans. and ed. David Walford with Ralf Meerbote. Cambridge: Cambridge University Press, 1992, p. 297.

2. Nietzsche, *Beyond Good and Evil*, trans. R. J. Hollingdale. Harmondsworth: Penguin, 1990, V, §186.

3. *Writings from the Late Notebooks*, trans. Kate Sturge. Cambridge: Cambridge University Press, 2003, 38[13], June–July 1885, p. 29.

4. *Just and Unjust Wars*, Preface to 1992 edition, pp. xxviii–xxix. On "we," some cautious thoughts are given by Michael J. Baxter, in "Dispelling the 'We' Fallacy," in Stanley Hauerwas and Frank Lentricchia, eds., *Dissent from the Homeland; Essays after September 11*. Durham: Duke University Press, 2003.

5. See p. 24.

6. See p. 30.

7. See p. 16.

8. *In Defence of History*, p. 52.

9. *Treatise of Human Nature*, 3.1.1,§26.

10. See p. 55.

11. Nietzsche, *Writings from the Late Notebooks*, 2[190] (1885–1886), pp. 95–96 [*eine Auslegung, eine Art zu interpretieren*]; *On the Genealogy of Morality*, III, §12.

12. "Physics in the Contemporary World," p. 67, see earlier p. 73.

13. The phrase is from Williams, *Ethics and the Limits of Philosophy*, p. 212n7, writing of Singer.

14. *Shame and Necessity*, p. 63.

15. *Ethical Studies*, p. 41.

16. T, p. 236.

17. *Ethical Studies*, p. 5.

18. "Physics in the Contemporary World," p. 66, see earlier p. 9; *The Journals of David E. Lilienthal*, vol. 2, *The Atomic Energy Years 1945–1950* (New York: Harper and Row, 1964), December 11, 1946, p. 118.

19. *Autrement qu'être*, pp. 141, 180, see pp. 89.

20. Earlier, p. 105.

21. See p. 119.

22. See n18.

23. See p 82.

24. See Bernard Williams, "The Point of View of the Universe: Sidgwick and the Ambitions of Ethics," in *Making Sense of Humanity*. Cambridge: Cambridge University Press, 1995.

25. See p. 39.

26. See p. 55.

27. See p. 24, from 1943.

28. See p. 19.

29. See p. 3.

REFERENCES

BIOGRAPHICAL BACKGROUND

A number of useful biographies of Oppenheimer appeared around the centenary of his birth. The most comprehensive is Kai Bird and Martin J. Sherwin, *American Prometheus: The Triumph and Tragedy of J. Robert Oppenheimer* (New York: Knopf, 2005). There is also David C. Cassidy, *Oppenheimer and the American Century* (New York: Pi Press, 2005) and Jeremy Bernstein, *Oppenheimer: Portrait of an Enigma* (Chicago: Ivan R. Dee, 2004). Alice Kimball Smith and Charles Weiner, *Robert Oppenheimer: Letters and Recollections* (Stanford: Stanford University Press, 1995) provides essential published documentation.

WORKS CITED

No details are given for standard works where any edition or translation may be used.

Adorno, Theodor, and Horkheimer, Max. *Dialectic of Enlightenment* (1944). Trans. John Cumming. London: Verso, 1995.
Alperovitz, Gar. *Atomic Diplomacy*. London: Secker & Warburg, 1966.
Anscombe, G. E. M. *Intention*. Oxford: Blackwell, 1957.
———. "Modern Moral Philosophy." *Philosophy*, 33, 1958.
Arendt, Hannah. *Eichmann in Jerusalem*. Harmondsworth: Penguin, 1976.
———. "Collective Responsibility," in *Responsibility and Judgment*. New York: Schocken, 2003.
Augustine. *Confessions*. Trans. Henry Chadwick. Oxford: Oxford University Press, 1992.

Badash, Lawrence. *Scientists and the Development of Nuclear Weapons*. Atlantic Highlands, NJ: Humanities Press, 1995.

Barkan, Elazar. *The Guilt of Nations: Restitution and Negotiating Historical Injustices*. New York: Norton, 2000.

Baxter, Michael J. "Dispelling the 'We' Fallacy," in Stanley Hauerwas and Frank Lentricchia, eds. *Dissent from the Homeland; Essays after September 11*. Durham: Duke University Press, 2003.

Bernstein, Jeremy. *Hitler's Uranium Club: The Secret Recordings at Farm Hall*. Woodbury NY: American Institute of Physics, 1996.

———. "Creators of the Bomb"(Review of Schweber, *In the Shadow of the Bomb*). *New York Review of Books*, May 11, 2000.

Blackett, P. M. S. *Military and Political Consequences of Atomic Energy*. London: Turnstile Press, 1948 (in United States: *Fear, War, and the Bomb*).

Boyer, Paul. *By the Bomb's Early Light: American Thought and Culture at the Dawn of the Atomic Age*. New York: Pantheon Books, 1985.

———. *Fallout*. Columbus: Ohio State University Press, 1998.

Bradley, Francis Herbert. "The Vulgar Notion of Responsibility" (1876), in *Ethical Studies*. Oxford: Oxford University Press, 1970.

Bukovsky, Vladimir. *To Build a Castle*. London: Deutsch, 1978.

Bush, Vannevar. *Modern Arms and Free Men*. London: Heinemann, 1950.

Clark, Maudmarie. *Nietzsche on Truth and Philosophy*. Cambridge: Cambridge University Press, 1990

Davis, Nuel Pharr. *Lawrence and Oppenheimer*. London: Cape, 1969.

Descartes, René. *Philosophical Writings*. Trans. J. Cottingham, R. Stoothoff, D. Murdoch. Cambridge: Cambridge University Press, 1985.

Epictetus. *Discourses*. Trans. E. Carter, revised R. Hard. London: Everyman, 1995.

Evans, Richard J. *In Defence of History*. London: Granta, 1997.

Fackenheim, Emil L. "The Holocaust and Philosophy." *Journal of Philosophy*, 82/10, October 1985.

Feynman, Richard. *The Meaning of It All*. London: Allen Lane, 1998.

———. Minority Report to the Space Shuttle *Challenger* Inquiry, in *The Pleasure of Finding Things Out*. London: Allen Lane, 2000.

Fischer, John Martin, and Ravizza, Mark. *Responsibility and Control: A Theory of Moral Responsibility*. Cambridge: Cambridge University Press, 1998.

Frayn, Michael. *Copenhagen* (with Postscript). London: Methuen, 1998.

French, Peter A. *Collective and Corporate Responsibility*. New York: Columbia University Press, 1984.

Gellner, Ernest. *Language and Solitude: Wittgenstein, Malinowski and the Habsburg Dilemma*. Cambridge: Cambridge University Press, 1998.

Glover, Jonathan. *Responsibility*. London: Routledge, 1970.

———. *Humanity: A Moral History of the Twentieth Century*. London: Cape, 1999.

Graham, Keith. *Practical Reasoning in a Social World*. Cambridge: Cambridge University Press, 2002.

Groves, Leslie R. *Now It Can be Told: The Story of the Manhattan Project.* London: Deutsch, 1963.

Geuss, Raymond. *Public Goods, Private Goods.* Princeton: Princeton University Press, 2001.

Habermas, Jürgen. "The Scientization of Politics and Public Opinion," from *Technik und Wissenschaft als 'Ideologie.'* Frankfurt: Suhrkamp Verlag, 1968. Trans. J. J. Shapiro in *Toward a Rational Society.* London: Heinemann, 1971.

Hardy, G. H. *A Mathematician's Apology* (1940). Cambridge: Cambridge University Press, 1992.

Hare, R. M. *Freedom and Reason.* Oxford: Oxford University Press, 1963.

———. "Rules of War and Moral Reasoning," *Philosophy and Public Affairs,* 1, 2, 1972.

Havel, Václav. *Letters to Olga.* Trans. Paul Wilson. London: Faber and Faber, 1990.

Hawkins, David. *Manhattan District History: Project Y: The Los Alamos Project,* vol. 1, *Inception until August 1945.* Los Alamos: Los Alamos Scientific Laboratory Report LAMS-2532, vol. 1, December 1, 1961 (reprinted with a new Introduction, Los Angeles/San Francisco: Tomash, 1983).

Heidegger, Martin. *Being and Time* (1927). Trans. Joan Stambaugh. Albany: State University of New York Press, 1996.

———. *The Question Concerning Technology* (1950). Trans. Willam Lovitt. New York: Harper, 1977.

Hijiya, James A. "The *Gita* of J. Robert Oppenheimer." *Proceedings of the American Philosophical Society,* 144, No. 2, June 2000.

Hoddeson, Lillian, Paul W. Henriksen, Roger A Meade, Catherine Westfall et al. *Critical Assembly: A Technical History of Los Alamos during the Oppenheimer Years, 1943–1945.* Cambridge: Cambridge University Press, 1993.

Holmes, Oliver Wendell. "Codes, and the Arrangement of the Law." *American Law Review,* 5, 1, 1870, in S. M. Novick ed., *Collected Works of Justice Holmes.* Chicago: University of Chicago Press, 1995, vol. 1.

Holton, Gerald. "Heisenberg, Oppenheimer, and Modern Physics" in *The Advancement of Science, and Its Burdens.* Cambridge: Cambridge University Press, 1986.

Honderich, Ted. *Philosopher: A Kind of Life.* London: Routledge, 2001,

Hooker, Brad, and Little, Margaret, eds. *Moral Particularism.* Oxford: Clarendon Press, 2000.

Hume, David. *Essays.* Oxford: Oxford University Press, 1963.

———. *An Enquiry concerning the Principles of Morals* (1751). Tom L. Beauchamp, ed. Oxford: Oxford University Press, 1998.

Johnson, Samuel. *The Life of Mr Richard Savage* (1744), in *Johnson: Prose and Poetry,* Mona Wilson, ed. London: Hart-Davis, 1970.

Jokic, Aleksandar, ed. *War Crimes and Collective Wrongdoings.* Oxford: Blackwell, 2001.

Jonsen, A. R., and Toulmin, S. *The Abuse of Casuistry: A History of Moral Reasoning*. Berkeley: University of Chicago Press, 1988.

Jungk, Robert. *Brighter than a Thousand Suns* (1956). Trans. James Cleugh. Harmondsworth: Penguin, 1960.

Kant, Immanuel. *Theoretical Philosophy 1755–1770*. David Walford with Ralf Meerbote trans. and ed. Cambridge: Cambridge University Press, 1992.

———. *Religion and Rational Theology*. Allen W. Wood and G. di Giovanni trans. and ed. Cambridge: Cambridge University Press, 1996.

———. *Practical Philosophy*. Mary J. Gregor trans. and ed. Cambridge: Cambridge University Press, 1996.

———. *Lectures on Ethics*. Peter Heath and J. B. Schneewind, eds. Cambridge: Cambridge University Press, 1997.

———. *Critique of Pure Reason* (1781/1787). Paul Guyer and Allen W. Wood trans. Cambridge: Cambridge University Press, 1998.

Keynes, John Maynard. *General Theory of Employment, Interest and Money* (1936). London: Macmillan, 1964.

Kitcher, Philip. *Science, Truth, and Democracy*. Oxford: Oxford University Press, 2001.

Levinas, Emmanuel. *Totalité et Infini*. Paris: Livres de Poche, 1971.

———. "Sans identité" in *L'humanisme de l'autre homme* (1978). Paris: Livres de Poche, nd.

———. *Autrement qu'être ou au-delà de l'essence*. Paris: Livres de Poche, 1996.

Lilienthal, David E. *The Journals of David E. Lilienthal*, vol. 2, *The Atomic Energy Years* 1945–1950. New York: Harper and Row, 1964.

Lilla, Mark. *The Reckless Mind: Intellectuals in Politics*. New York: NYRB, 2001.

MacCulloch, Diarmaid. *Reformation: Europe's House Divided 1490–1700*. London: Allen Lane, 2003.

MacKenzie, Donald, and Spinardi, Graham. "Tacit Knowledge and the Uninvention of Nuclear Weapons," in D. MacKenzie, ed. *Knowing Machines: Essays on Technical Change*. Cambridge: MIT Press, 1996.

Malebranche, Nicholas. *The Search after Truth* (1674/5). T. M Lennon trans. Cambridge: Cambridge University Press, 1997.

McCarthy, Mary. Letter to *Politics*. November 1946, p. 367.

Montaigne, Michel de. *An Apology for Raymond Sebond* (1569). M. A. Screech trans. Harmondsworth: Penguin, 1987.

Moore, G. E. "Certainty," in *Philosophical Papers*. London: Allen & Unwin, 1959.

Murdoch, Iris. "The Idea of Perfection" (1962), in *Existentialists and Mystics*. Peter Conradi, ed. London: Chatto and Windus, 1997.

Nagel, T. "War and Massacre," in *Philosophy and Public Affairs*, 1, 2, 1972.

———. *Mortal Questions*. Cambridge: Cambridge University Press, 1979.

———. *Other Minds*. Oxford: Oxford University Press, 1995.

———. *The Last Word*. New York: Oxford, 1997.

Nietzsche, Friedrich. *The Gay Science* (1882/1887). Trans. Josefine Nauckhoff. Cambridge: Cambridge University Press, 2001.

———. *Thus Spoke Zarathustra* (1883/1885). Trans. R. J. Hollingdale. Harmondsworth: Penguin, 1969.

———. *Beyond Good and Evil* (1886). Trans. R. J. Hollingdale. Harmondsworth: Penguin, 1990.

———. *On the Genealogy of Morality* (1887). Trans. Keith Ansell-Pearson. Cambridge: Cambridge University Press, 1994.

———. *Writings from the Late Notebooks*. Trans. Kate Sturge. Cambridge: Cambridge University Press, 2003.

O'Neill, Onora. "Reason and Politics in the Kantian Enterprise" and "The power of example," in *Constructions of Reason*. Cambridge: Cambridge University Press, 1989.

Operation Epsilon: The Farm Hall Transcripts. Bristol and Philadelphia: Institute of Physics Publishing, 1993.

Oppenheimer, J. Robert. "Atomic Weapons." *Proceedings of the American Philosophical Society*, 90, no. 1, 1946.

———. "Physics in the Contemporary World." *Bulletin of the Atomic Scientists*, vol. 4, no. 3, 1948 (also in *Technology Review*, 50, 1948).

———. "Encouragement of Science." *Bulletin of the Atomic Scientists*, January 1951.

———. *Atom and Void*. Princeton: Princeton University Press, 1989.

Patočka, Jan. *Heretical Essays in the Philosophy of History*. Trans. Erazim Kohák. Chicago: Open Court, 1996.

Perutz, Max F. "Why Did the Germans Not Make the Bomb?," in *I Wish I'd Made You Angrier Earlier*. Oxford: Oxford University Press, 1998.

Plato. *Republic*. G. M. A. Grube trans. C. D. C. Reeve rev. in *Complete Works*, ed. J. M. Cooper. Indianapolis: Hackett, 1997.

Rabi, I. I. et al. *Oppenheimer*. New York: Scribner's, 1969.

Rhodes, Richard. *The Making of the Atomic Bomb*. Harmondsworth: Penguin, 1986.

Rigden, John S. *Rabi: Scientist and Citizen*. New York: Basic Books, 1987.

Rorty, R. "On Heidegger's Nazism," in *Philosophy and Social Hope*. London: Penguin, 1999.

Ross, Paul Lawrence. *Heisenberg and the Nazi Atomic Bomb Project: A Study in German Culture*. Berkeley: University of California Press, 1998.

Rotblat, Joseph. "Leaving the Bomb Project." *Bulletin of the Atomic Scientists*, vol. 41, no.7, August 1985.

Sakharov, Andrei. *Memoirs*. Trans. Richard Lourie. New York: Knopf, 1990.

Schweber, S. S. *In the Shadow of the Bomb: Oppenheimer, Bethe, and the Responsibility of the Scientist*. Princeton: Princeton University Press, 2000.

Sebald, W. G. *On the Natural History of Destruction*. Trans. Anthea Bell. London: Hamish Hamilton, 2003.

Sereny, Gitta. *Into that Darkness* (1974). London: Pimlico, 1995.

Sherwin, Martin. *A World Destroyed: The Atomic Bomb and the Grand Alliance*. New York: Knopf, 1975.

Skidelsky, Robert. *John Maynard Keynes*, vol. 3. London: Macmillan, 2000.

Smith, Adam. *The Theory of Moral Sentiments* (1759). Eds. D. D. Raphael and A. L. Macfie. Indianapolis: Liberty Fund reprint, 1984.

Smith, Alice Kimball. *A Peril and a Hope: The Scientists' Movement in America, 1945–1947*. Chicago: University of Chicago Press, 1965.

Smith, Alice Kimball, and Weiner, Charles. *Robert Oppenheimer: Letters and Recollections*. Stanford: Stanford University Press, 1995.

Spinoza, Benedictus de. *Ethics* and *Treatise on the Emendation of the Intellect*. Trans. S. Shirley. Indianapolis: Hackett, 1992.

———. *Political Treatise*. Trans. S. Shirley. Indianapolis: Hackett, 2000.

Singer, Peter. *Rethinking Life and Death*. New York: St Martin's Press, 1995.

Stoff, M. B., Fanton, J. F., and Williams, R. H. *The Manhattan Project: A Documentary Introduction to the Atomic Age*. Philadelphia: Temple University Press, 1991.

Taylor, Charles. *Sources of the Self*. Cambridge: Cambridge University Press, 1989.

Teller, Edward. "Atomic Scientists Have Two Responsibilities." *Bulletin of the Atomic Scientists*, vol. 3 no 12, 1947.

———. (with A. Brown). *The Legacy of Hiroshima*. London: Macmillan, 1962.

——— (with Judith Shoolery). *Memoirs*. Cambridge: Perseus, 2001.

Tiles, M., and Oberdiek, H. *Living in a Technological Culture*. London: Routledge, 1995.

Tönnies, Ferdinand. *Community and Civil Society* (1887). Jose Harris trans. Cambridge: Cambridge University Press, 2001.

Toulmin, Stephen. *Cosmopolis*. Chicago: University of Chicago Press, 1992.

United States Atomic Energy Commission. *In the Matter of J. Robert Oppenheimer: Transcript of Hearing Before Personnel Security Board, Washington DC, April 12, 1954, through May 6, 1954*. Washington DC: U.S. Government Printing Office, 1954.

Walzer, Michael. *Just and Unjust Wars*. New York: Basic Books, 2nd ed. 1992.

Williams, B. "Internal and External Reasons," in *Moral Luck*. Cambridge: Cambridge University Press, 1981.

———. "Morality, Scepticism and the Nuclear Arms Race," in N. Blake and K. Pole eds. *Objections to Nuclear Defence*. London: Routledge, 1984.

———. *Ethics and the Limits of Philosophy*. London: Fontana, 1985.

———. *Shame and Necessity*. Berkeley: University of California Press, 1993.

———. "The Point of View of the Universe: Sidgwick and the Ambitions of Ethics," in *Making Sense of Humanity*. Cambridge: Cambridge University Press, 1995.

———. *Truth and Truthfulness*. Princeton: Princeton University Press, 2002.
Williams, Robert C., and Cantelon, Philip L. eds. *The American Atom: A Documentary History of Nuclear Policies from the Discovery of Nuclear Fission to the Present 1939–1984*. Philadelphia: University of Pennsylvania Press, 1984.
Wittgenstein, Ludwig. *Culture and Value*, ed. G. H. von Wright, trans. Peter Winch. Oxford: Blackwell, 1984.

INDEX